"Preaching is the rudder of the church; it p　　　　　　　　　　the raw material the Holy Spirit uses to transform lives. Every honest pastor wants to become a more powerful and effective communicator and Sunukjian's Biblical Preaching for the Contemporary Church series is one of the most effective tools I know. His coaching and example have had a significant role in shaping how I teach God's word today and I highly recommend his work to you."

—**Chip Ingram,** Senior Pastor, Venture Christian Church;
Teaching Pastor, Living on the Edge

"These model sermons remind us that exposition should be interesting, relevant, and at the same time thoroughly biblical. These messages should not just be read by pastors, but by anyone who wants their soul blessed by the transforming truth of the Scriptures."

—**Erwin W. Lutzer,** Senior Pastor, The Moody Church

"We are living in a day when Bible exposition has fallen on hard times. There are too few models and even fewer practitioners. Sunukjian is one of the best at wedding solid biblical exposition with creative and relevant applications. His artful use of imagination and penetrating questions in connecting the listener to the text is an invaluable guide for faithfully preaching the ever true and practical Word of God."

—**Mark L. Bailey,** President and Professor of Bible Exposition,
Dallas Theological Seminary

"Good preaching is both a science and an art. While it is relatively easy to master the science of exegesis, the final product is wrapped in the far more challenging art of application, illustration, and delivery. I've found that being exposed to communicators who do the art well has been both instructional and inspirational. This book is full of outstanding examples of sermons that excel in both science and art. If it is true that great preaching is not only taught, but caught, then reading through these sermons will be a significant help in upgrading the effectiveness of your preaching!"

—**Joseph M. Stowell,** President, Cornerstone University

"Sunukjian is not only an influential teacher of preachers; he's also an outstanding biblical expositor. In his exceptional new Biblical Preaching for the Contemporary Church series, Sunukjian wears both hats and helps his readers become more effective biblical communicators as he demonstrates excellent examples of contemporary expository preaching. His sermons are filled with fascinating illustrations and timely application while also reflecting powerful insights into the biblical text. These are books that will encourage any reader—pastor or layperson—and they deserve a place on any preacher's bookshelf."

—**Michael Duduit,** Executive Editor, *Preaching* magazine;
Dean, College of Christian Studies and the Clamp Divinity School,
Anderson University

"Some things can best be taught; others are better caught than taught. Good preaching requires both, which is why we should all be grateful for the unique combination found in Sunukjian's textbook, *Invitation to Biblical Preaching,* and now his Biblical Preaching for the Contemporary Church series. The instruction and examples provided by this veteran expositor and teacher of expositors are unmatched in their usefulness to preachers everywhere."

—**Duane Litfin,** President Emeritus, Wheaton College

"Much ink has been spilled in recent years on matters homiletical. These works have been mostly theoretical and some exhortative, but hardly any modeling of sermons. Sunukjian has done the church and the pastorate a service with his carefully thought out expository sermons in this series of books. The preacher who has an ear will harken to these examples from the pen of a master preacher and teacher of preachers—well worth the investment of one's time. It will sharpen your skills, spark your creativity, and shape your productions in the pulpit, for the glory of God and the edification of his people."

—**Abraham Kuruvilla,** Professor of Pastoral Ministries,
Dallas Theological Seminary

"The best way to learn how to preach well is to copy the masters. Sunukjian's Biblical Preaching for the Contemporary Church series puts into print a wealth of biblical expositions that are worth imitating. Fulsome, gripping introductions draw the reader into the life issue which the text of Scripture—and therefore the sermon—addresses. Ideas flow logically, just as one would expect from the author of *Invitation to Biblical Preaching,* where Sunukjian demonstrates unparalleled mastery of that skill. The content of each sermon is well-researched but it doesn't sound overly academic. Sermons reflect the preaching portion's contribution to the biblical book being expounded. The oral style is engaging and the illustrations not only clarify ideas, they shed the light of Scripture on us who hear them. These volumes will do preachers who read them a lot of good—so long as they learn from the preacher and resist the temptation to copy his sermons!"

—**Greg R. Scharf,** Professor of Pastoral Theology, Trinity Evangelical Divinity School

"Nearly everything I learned about sermon preparation and delivery, I learned from my former preaching professor Don Sunukjian. His new series Biblical Preaching for the Contemporary Church is a must-read for every preacher and teacher who desires to effectively communicate God's timeless truths."

—**Robert Jeffress,** Pastor, First Baptist Church, Dallas, Texas

"From my first bite into the meaty-yet-accessible volumes of Sunukjian's Biblical Preaching for the Contemporary Church series, I was taught and touched by its blend of solidity in depth with insight in content, bringing together an enriching immediate practicality."

—**Jack Hayford,** Founder and Chancellor, The King's University

BIBLICAL PREACHING
FOR THE CONTEMPORARY CHURCH

Invitation to Philippians:
  Building a Great Church through Humility

Invitation to James:
  Persevering through Trials to Win the Crown

Invitation to the Life of Jacob:
  Winning through Losing

Invitation to Galatians
  (forthcoming)

Invitation to Mark
  (forthcoming)

Invitation to Joshua
  (forthcoming)

INVITATION TO PHILIPPIANS

BUILDING A GREAT CHURCH through HUMILITY

DONALD R. SUNUKJIAN

LEXHAM PRESS

Invitation to Philippians: Building a Great Church through Humility
© 2014 by Donald R. Sunukjian

Lexham Press, 1313 Commercial St., Bellingham, WA 98225
LexhamPress.com

First edition by Weaver Book Company.

Print ISBN 9781683592228
Digital ISBN 9781683592235

Cover design: LUCAS Art & Design
Editorial, design, and production:
      { In a Word } www.inawordbooks.com
      /edited by Daphne Parsekian/

To the wonderful folks at
The Armenian Christian Fellowship
of Orange County;
no pastor was ever more loved.

CONTENTS

SERIES PREFACE

Some years ago I wrote a textbook—*Invitation to Biblical Preaching*—which has been translated into several languages and is being used rather widely to develop biblical preachers. This current series of volumes is being published as an *Invitation* to sermons on specific biblical books, individuals, or themes. The purpose of this series is to offer models of the principles presented in the textbook.

A sermon comes alive when it is true to the biblical author's flow of thought, clear in its unfolding, interesting to listen to, and connected to contemporary life. Hopefully that's true of the messages in this book.

These messages were originally preached before a congregation of God's people, and then slightly edited to their present form in order to adjust from the *hearing ear* to the *reading eye*. But I've tried my best to retain their oral flavor—I've wanted them to still sound close to the way we talk. This means there will be incomplete sentences, colloquial and idiomatic language, and other features of the spoken word.

I've also occasionally included some *stage directions,* so that the reader can visualize any props or large physical movements that were part of a message.

May God speak to your heart through his Word.

INTRODUCTION

The church at Philippi was probably the one Paul loved the most. Every time he remembered them, he thanked God for them (1:3). They were dear to his heart, and he longed for them with all the affection of Christ (1:7–8).

They were the only church that supported him financially. At the end of his first visit to them, they sent him on his further missionary travels with a parting gift (4:15) and then repeatedly followed that up with additional financial aid (4:16). One of the reasons he wrote this letter was because Epaphroditus, one of their members, had just brought him yet another sizeable gift (1:3–5; 4:10–18).

The money Epaphroditus had brought enabled Paul to pay his living expenses. When he wrote, he was under house arrest in Rome, chained to a guard, though with freedom of movement through the house. He was financially responsible, however, for the rent on the house and for his food. If his funds dried up, the alternative would be a damp dungeon with little food and unhealthy conditions. In part, therefore, this is a thank-you letter to the Philippians for their generous and helpful gift.

Paul also had other reasons for writing. He had heard that the Philippian Christians were suffering for the faith, and he wanted to encourage them (1:27–30; 3:17–4:1). He had also heard of dissension in the church. Instead of humbly deferring to one another, some were insisting on having their own way (2:1–4; 4:2–5). He spent much of his letter pointing them to the examples set by Christ (2:1–11) and himself (3:3–16). In addition, he held up Timothy and Epaphroditus, two men well known to them, as models of self-sacrificing love (2:19–30).

It's understandable that the Philippian church would struggle with issues of pride and self-importance. The city of Philippi had a unique, special status—it was a colony of Rome. This meant that even though it was located eight hundred miles from Rome, it was as though its citizens lived in Rome itself, with all the rights and privileges of Roman citizenship. Their pride in their Roman citizenship influenced their behavior in the church. Paul reminded the believers that they were most of all citizens of heaven (1:27; 3:17–4:1) and that they needed to live worthy of this higher allegiance.

Paul structured his letter to the Philippians in a *chiastic* pattern (see below), which means that his sequential top and bottom sections have matching themes and that his dominant section is the point of the wedge (>). In other words, Timothy and Epaphroditus, on a human level, model the exact spirit of humility and self-sacrifice that Paul wanted to see in the Philippians (2:19–30).

A   Opening greetings (1:1–2)

    B   Thanks for your gift; my prayer for you (1:3–11)

        C   Rising above disunity and difficulty by rejoicing in Christ (1:12–26)

            D   Standing firm as citizens; contending together (1:27–30)

                E   In humility, living like Christ (2:1–11)

                    F   Becoming blameless and pure (2:12–18)

                        G   Timothy and Epaphroditus (2:19–30)

                    F'   Guarding against evil men (3:1–4)

                E'   In humility, living for Christ (3:5–16)

            D'   Standing firm as citizens; waiting for the Lord (3:17–4:1)

        C'   Rising above disunity and difficulty by rejoicing in the Lord (4:2–7)

    B'   Thanks for your gift; my desire for you (4:8–20)

A'   Final greetings (4:21–23)

The benefit of a chiastic structure is that it helps the reader to anticipate the flow of thought and to more accurately understand the matching sections in light of each other.

1

THE BLAZING FASTBALL THAT GIVES US CONFIDENCE

Philippians 1:1–8

July 15, 1986, Roger Clemens went to bat in his first all-star game. Roger was the sizzling right-hander for the Boston Red Sox who had been named starting pitcher for the American League All-Star team. In the second inning, it was his turn to bat. But batting was something Roger Clemens was not used to doing. He never batted, because in his league, the American League, they had the designated-hitter rule—someone else batted in place of the pitcher. Roger Clemens never batted; he just pitched. But the All-Star games between the American League and the National League alternated each year between the rules of the two leagues, and this year it was the National League's rule—pitchers would bat for themselves. So Roger Clemens found himself coming to bat for the first time.

He took a few uncertain practice swings in the on-deck circle, and then he stepped into the batter's box. On the mound was Dwight Gooden, the best pitcher in the National League. The year before, Dwight had won the Cy Young Award for being the best pitcher in all of baseball. So a pitcher who never batted was facing the best pitcher in all of baseball.

Dwight Gooden wound up and threw a white-hot, streaking fastball that blew by Roger Clemens. Roger stepped out of the box and blinked his eyes a few times. Then he turned to the catcher behind him, Gary Carter. "Gary, is that what *my* pitches look like?"

"You bet it is!" Gary said.

Roger Clemens stepped back into the box and quickly struck out. But when he went back on the pitcher's mound to pitch for his team, he threw three perfect innings—nobody on the other team got a hit. He was voted the game's Most Valuable Player. And he told people that from that day on, he had a greater confidence in his own pitching. When he saw how powerful his own fastball was and when he saw how it was working, he then pitched with all the confidence in the world.

What could give a church that same confidence—that God was powerfully working in it? What streaking "fastball" could we see that would tell us that God was making our church a place of joy and spiritual growth?

That's not just a question for a church. It's also a question for individuals. What would give *you* confidence that God was genuinely working in *you*? What "fastball" would give you confidence that he's part of your life, actively working in you, and planning nothing but good for you?

What gives churches or individuals confidence that God is working in them?

One day, sitting in prison, the apostle Paul wrote to a church, "I'm *confident* that God has begun a *good work* in you, and I'm confident that he'll continue that work until it's complete. I'm absolutely confident that God has started something good in you, and I know for sure he's going to finish it."

What made him say that? What did he see in that small Philippian church that led him to write, "Being confident of this, that he who began a good work in you will carry it on to completion until the day of Christ Jesus" (1:6)?

Paul was confident; he was absolutely sure that God had started something very good in this small church—God had brought them into existence, and he was now working in them to accomplish something very good; nothing was going to stop it from taking place. What made Paul so confident? What made him so sure?

The reason Paul was so confident was because he saw some very concrete, objective, consistent things they were doing so that others would hear about what Christ had done for them. Look at the opening paragraphs of his letter to see that this is what gives us confidence that God is at work in us—because we're doing some very tangible and on-going things to make Christ known to others.

> *Paul and Timothy, servants of Christ Jesus, to all God's holy people in Christ Jesus at Philippi, together with the overseers and deacons: Grace and peace to you from God our Father and the Lord Jesus Christ. I thank my God every time I remember you. In all my prayers for all of you, I always pray with joy because of your partnership in the gospel.* (1:1–5a)

There it is—"your partnership in the gospel"—your tangible joining with me in making Christ known to others. I'm thankful for your partnership, for all the objective, concrete things you're doing so that others can hear about Christ.

Paul goes on to say that this tangible partnership has been ongoing—"from the first day until now"—"from when we first met until just this last week." It's not only been concrete, it's been sustained and consistent over the years. It's been a partnership in the gospel over a long period of time.

This tangible, sustained partnership in making the gospel known is what makes Paul confident that God is working in them—"being confident of this, that he who began a good work in you will carry it on to completion until the day of Christ Jesus" (1:6). Your tangible and ongoing partnership in the gospel, the things you do so that others will hear about him, concretely showing up over a long period of time—these are the things that make me confident God has started something in you and he's going to carry it to completion.

Paul is justified in having this confidence about them:

> *It is right for me to feel this way about all of you, since I have you in my heart and, whether I am in chains or defending and confirming the gospel, all of you share in God's grace with me. God can testify how I long for all of you with the affection of Christ Jesus.* (1:7–8)

He affectionately has them in his heart; he loves them and knows their history. He remembers them with joy because whether he is in chains, as he is presently, or whether he is out and about, they have continually and tangibly partnered with him in the grace of making Christ known to others.

What was Paul remembering? What was their tangible and on-going commitment to share with him in making the gospel known? What concrete actions reveal that a church or individual is committed to making Christ known? He undoubtedly has three things in mind.

First, their homes were available as a place to meet. "From the very first day" he met them, one of them immediately made her home available as a regular meeting place. Right off the bat, there was a spirit of "Please, use my home as a place where others can come and hear the message." He remembered his first week in the city and how the first person to accept the gospel tangibly made it possible for others to also hear the good news.

We know about this immediate opening of the home from the book of Acts, where we read about Paul's first week in their city. He came to their city on one of his missionary travels. There were no Christians in the city at that time. It fact, there weren't even enough Jews in the city to have a Jewish synagogue. The best Paul could find was a small Jewish prayer meeting, mostly women, that met under some trees by the river. He joined them and began to speak about Christ to them. The Lord opened the heart of one of the ladies there, a woman named Lydia. Lydia owned her own import business and had a large house, which she immediately made available. She pressed Paul to use her home as a base for his ministry and wouldn't take "No" for an answer:

> From Troas we put out to sea and sailed straight for Samothrace, and the next day on to Neapolis. From there we traveled to Philippi, a Roman colony and the leading city of that district of Macedonia. And we stayed there several days. On the Sabbath we went outside the city gate to the river, where we expected to find a place of prayer. We sat down and began to speak to the women who had gathered there. One of those listening was a woman from the city of Thyatira named Lydia, a dealer in purple cloth. She was a worshiper of God. The Lord opened her heart to respond to Paul's message. When she and the members of her household were baptized, she invited us to her home. "If you consider me a

believer in the Lord," she said, "come and stay at my house." And she persuaded us. (Acts 16:11–15)

Paul continued in Philippi for a period of time, undergoing flogging and imprisonment as a result of his ministry. When he was finally released and ready to resume his travels, he said farewell to the believers at Lydia's house, which had continued to be a meeting place for the believers (Acts 16:16–40).

That's one way you can be confident that people are committed to the work of the Lord—their homes are available.

Obviously, not everybody's home is large enough for some gatherings. That was true in Philippi, and it's true with us. Lydia was in the import business and apparently made enough money to have a home that could accommodate others. Not all of us have that kind of home.

But when people do have suitable homes and quickly open them up for others, that's a sign that God is working in them. It shows that they're committed to participating in the ministry of making him known. They're willing to go through the effort of vacuuming the rugs, straightening the furniture, cleaning the windows, mowing the lawn, and making refreshments. You can be confident that God is working in them because you see a tangible desire to help God's work take place.

When people can't be bothered to make their homes available, it may be because the work of God is not central to their lives. Their attitude is: "Yes, go to church on Sunday, but after that, get on with life, and don't put yourself out anymore." It doesn't seem that God or his work is important to them.

You can be confident that God is working when homes are quickly available so that others can benefit.

What else was Paul remembering? What other tangible, ongoing evidence did he see that made him confident God was working in them?

He was remembering, secondly, that they were willing to take some heat for their faith. They knew they would pay a price in their culture if they became Christians, and they were willing to pay it.

Philippi was a unique city with a special government status, which we'll learn more about later. It was connected to the Roman emperor in ways other cities weren't. And it was important, therefore, in Philippi, to be politically correct, which meant worshipping the emperor as if he were a god. Paul remembered that his Christian friends in Philippi were willing to pay the price for not doing that. He'll say a little later in his letter, "You're going through some of the same stuff I had to go through; you're suffering some of the same things I did because of your Christian faith" (Phil. 1:28–30).

Their tangible, sustained partnership showed in their willingness to pay a price for their Christian faith. You can be confident that God is at work in someone when you see that person standing up for the truth and willing to take some heat for it.

When you see a young mom raise the question in a PTA meeting, "Do we really need to have 'alternative lifestyles' introduced into our 4th grade classes? I'm not sure I want my 10-year-old daughter to read a book titled *Johnny Has Two Daddies* or *Both My Mommies Love Me*. Is that necessary? I wish we wouldn't do that"—when you see her stand for the truth, even though it may mean being booed or hissed or called homophobic, narrow, and prejudiced—when you see someone willing to pay a price for the sake of the truth, you can be confident that God is in her, working something good in her life.

When you see an elderly widow and widower get married—both in their 80s, both living on Social Security, both knowing that if they just shacked up together, they could keep both their Social Security checks, but if they do the righteous thing and get married, our government will cancel one of their Social Security checks, and they'll have to live on half the money—when you see them take a stand for truth and righteousness and pay a price for it, you can be confident that God is part of their lives and doing good in them.

When people won't take a stand for the truth and when they won't risk some consequence for the sake of righteousness, it's probably because God is not part of their lives. He's not working in them. Their attitude is: "Never mind what God wants; I'm gonna look out for myself."

Paul says, "I remember your homes being available and your willingness to stand for the truth. And I'm confident that God has started a good work in you, which he'll take to completion."

There's one last thing that Paul was remembering. There's one more tangible, specific, concrete thing they did—consistently—from the first day right up until the time he wrote this letter. And it seemed to be uppermost in his mind, for he spent the most time on it. It more than anything else made him confident about them. It was that generously, again and again, they gave their money. You can have confidence that God is in people's lives when they give their money.

More than once these Philippians had sent money to Paul over the years to support him in his travels and preaching. The very letter he was then writing was in part a "thank you" note for their latest gift, one that had arrived just that week. More than anything else, their financial partnership and desire to share in the gospel convinced him that God was at work in them.

He will be explicit about this at the end of his letter. He's thankful that they've been been able to send another financial gift, not so much because he needs the money, but because of what it says about God's work in them:

> I rejoiced greatly in the Lord that at last you renewed your concern for me. Indeed, you were concerned, but you had no opportunity to show it. I am not saying this because I am in need, for I have learned to be content whatever the circumstances. I know what it is to be in need, and I know what it is to have plenty. I have learned the secret of being content in any and every situation, whether well fed or hungry, whether living in plenty or in want. I can do all this through him who gives me strength.
>
> Yet it was good of you to share in my troubles. Moreover, as you Philippians know, in the early days of your acquaintance with the gospel, when I set out from Macedonia, not one church shared with me in the matter of giving and receiving, except you only; for even when I was in Thessalonica, you sent me aid more than once when I was in need. Not that I desire your gifts; what I desire is that more be credited to your account. (4:10–17)

Paul remembers that from the first day until the present, they were the only church that partnered financially with him in making the gospel known. And this made him confident that God was at work in them. When people give money generously, again and again, you can be confident that God is in their lives.

When people won't do that—when they give just a few bucks to sort of play the part instead of the real percentage of their incomes that God is looking for—it's probably a sign that God is not in their lives. Because when God has begun a work in you and you sense his reality and his presence, you want to honor him. You want to thank him, and you want to give at a level that says, "I want others to know you too." When God is real and working in people's lives, they give—generously and consistently.

Paul remembered this small church's partnership from the first day he met them to the present. He remembered the tangible and ongoing things they did for the sake of the gospel—their homes being opened, their stand for the truth, and their consistent and generous giving. And he was confident that God had begun a good work in them and would take it to completion.

We can share that confidence that God is doing a good work in us. We can point to the same things. Not a streaking fastball, but the concrete and consistent things that we do: our homes opened for prayer, for youth, for meetings; our willingness to take a stand for the truth; and our loving and joyful giving in order that God's work will be strong.

2

CHOOSING WHAT IS BEST

Philippians 1:9–11

There were about twenty of us—the engaged couple, their parents, the bridesmaids and groomsmen who were going to be in the wedding the next day, and Nell and I. We were seated around a long table in the upstairs room of a Mexican restaurant for the joyful celebration dinner that follows a wedding rehearsal.

The bride's parents had been members of our church for about a year: Gary and Joanne—wonderful people. Only a year or two earlier they had become Christians. It was all new and exciting to them, and they were growing and serving the Lord. And now their daughter was marrying a fine Christian husband.

There was lots of laughter and fun at the table. I remember saying real loud to Gary so everybody else at the table could hear, "Hey, Gary. I asked a man once what it was like to give away his daughter in marriage. And he told me, 'It's like taking your finely tuned Stradivarius and handing it to a gorilla.'" Everyone laughed. Then the mother of the groom stood up: "I'm the mother of that gorilla, and I resent that." More laughter.

Just then the waitress brought in margaritas and set one down in front of everybody. When everybody had one, Gary rose with his margarita in hand to make a toast—a toast to the happiness of his daughter and her wonderful new husband. Some people around the table reached for their margaritas. Other people around the table looked down to see what I was doing. They were thinking, "Is it okay to drink alcohol? What will the pastor think? What should I do?"

Gary was finishing his toast. Some people were reaching. Other people were looking. And my mind was spinning fast: "Gary is absolutely innocent in what he's doing. To him as a new Christian, it's perfectly natural that he would toast his daughter with a margarita. If I don't join in, he and his wife will be mortified. They'll think they've made a terrible mistake, that they've done something terribly wrong. They'll worry that the pastor will forever look down on them. If I don't join in, they'll take it as my disapproval of them spiritually.

"But I know there are other people in the church who think it's a sin to drink alcohol. In their mind, Christians don't drink. If I *do* join in, they'll hear that I drank, and they'll think it's terrible—'The pastor drinks! What kind of a pastor is that?' And they'll sit in judgment of me and ignore my preaching from then on.

"What should I do? The toast is ending. People are reaching, looking. If I don't join in, I hurt Gary and Joanne. If I do join in, I hurt other people in the church. I need to make a choice. I need to make the best choice."

Situations like that come up all the time—where you need to make a choice and you want to make the best choice.

Occasionally, I get a phone call: "Pastor Sunukjian, you don't know me, but I've heard about you and your church. My fiancée and I want to get married. We're not really church people, but we'd still like a pastor to perform the ceremony. Would you be willing to do it?"

I need to make a choice, and I want it to be the best choice. One choice would be to say, "Yes," thinking that maybe, as we meet for several weeks of premarital counseling, I can win them to the Lord. Maybe they'll start coming to the church and grow in the Lord. One choice would be to say, "Paul, I'd be delighted to do that. Let's talk about some ways we can spend some time together before the wedding day."

The other choice would be to say, "Paul, I'm sorry, I'm just not able to do that. With my schedule, I just don't have the hours to be able to do that." And I would be thinking of how many hours it would take—hours for the premarital counseling, hours for the wedding rehearsal, hours for the wedding and celebration afterward. Do I have the hours for that? If I took the hours away from my other responsibilities—teaching at a seminary, pastoring a church—would something suffer in one of those ministries? Would I shortchange the students? Would someone in the church who wants to meet with me get put off because there was no time available?

One choice would be to say, "Yes," hoping to win this man and his fiancée to the Lord. The other choice would be to say, "No," because even though it might be a good thing, it would perhaps take away from other necessary things. I need to make a choice, and I want it to be the best choice.

These kinds of situations come up all the time—you need to make a choice, and you want it to be the best choice.

Should you buy your teenage son a car? Would he be a responsible driver? Would the cost of the car and the insurance be so much that it would hurt other areas of the family finances? On the one hand, providing him with a car would help him get to school and around to his activities, saving hours of chauffeuring by others in the family. On the other hand, would it be spoiling him, giving him something for nothing? Should he have to pay for the gas, the insurance? Should he be expected to drive younger brothers and sisters to their activities?

Should you buy your child a car? Would it be good for him, for the family? What would be the best choice?

Your adult sister seems to be going through a difficult time. Some trauma has occurred in her life—a divorce, a death, the loss of a job, deterioration in health. You comfort her, you support her, you listen to her, you encourage her, you help her out. Months later, she hasn't gotten any better; she doesn't seem to have recovered in any way. She's still acting needy; she's still carrying her hurt and burdening others with her sorrow.

Is she still really struggling with her emotions and healing, or is she just selfishly hanging on to the wound because it makes others pay attention to her? Does she need more compassion and more time? Or does she need a kick in the rear and a "Snap out of it!"? Should you hug her or shake her? Should you comfort and encourage her or give her a dose of reality? Which should you choose? What would be best?

These kinds of situations come up all the time. They come up in church.

Someone at church makes a comment. You're not sure how to take it. Was it kind of a jab at you? Or was it totally unintentional and innocent?

Should you address it and clear the air? Or should you let it go and assume the person meant nothing by it? What would be the best choice?

One of the kids in the Sunday school or youth group is acting up. You're the teacher or the leader. Should you manage as best as you can for the sake of the child and the family? Or for the sake of the others in the group, should you ask him to leave, perhaps offending the family? Which should you choose? What would be best?

One of the young couples in the church decides that God is calling them to be missionaries overseas. They've signed up with a mission board, and now they're raising support. They need to raise about $4,000 a month—to cover transportation, language school, living expenses, and mission overhead costs. They come to the elders of their home church, hoping that the church will support them financially, maybe even to the level of $1,000 a month. The other $3,000 will hopefully come from friends, family, and other churches.

The elders interview them and then meet privately to decide. Based on the interview, the couple doesn't seem very well prepared for missionary work. They lack training. There seem to be some significant areas of spiritual immaturity. They haven't served much in the church. Nor have they shown much diligence or hard work in secular employment. But they've grown up in the church, and they both have families who are active in the church. Is this the call of God that will finally bring purpose and direction to their lives? Does the church have sufficient, steady income to commit $1,000 a month for the next ten years? Would it be more beneficial for the life of the church to hire a part-time youth pastor with that money or to commit it to these young missionaries? What would be the best choice?

These kinds of situations come up all the time—you need to make a choice, and you want it to be the best choice.

How can we know what the best choice is in these situations—whether to drink the alcohol, perform the marriage, buy the car, comfort the family member, address the comment, discipline the kid, or support the young couple? How can we know what is the best choice in a situation where there are all kinds of factors, different options, and conflicting possibilities? What will help us to choose what is best?

In the early days of Christianity, the apostle Paul was thinking about his friends in a church he loved. He was absolutely confident that God was at work in them. They were his partners in the gospel. He saw them doing some very tangible and ongoing things to make God known to others, and he loved them more than he loved any other church.

But he also knew they were facing some choices—choices about how to handle certain situations. Some situations involved people who were teaching in the church. Others involved how some of the members of the church were acting toward each other. Still other situations were developing in the community or culture at large. There were different ways his friends in the church could go on each of these situations. They would have to make some choices, and he wanted them to choose what was best.

So he writes to them, telling them why it's important that they choose wisely and what will enable them to do so. He says, "I want you to *discern what is best* (Phil. 1:10). I want you to pick the best course of action in any situation." He first tells them why they should be concerned about making the best choice and then what will make it possible for them to do that.

Why is it important to make the best choice? Two reasons: First, so that no one else will have anything against us, and second, so that we ourselves will know that we've pleased God in every way.

The first reason is so that no one else will have anything against us or feel we've acted incorrectly. That's what Paul means when he writes, "I want you to discern what is best so that you may be pure and blameless for the day of Christ" (Phil. 1:10)—so that others will see that you acted with sincerity and integrity and that you did nothing deliberately to hurt them, but instead had their best interests at heart.

When Paul writes that he wants them to be *pure*, he uses a word in their culture that means "without wax." In that part of the world, they used to make beautiful, delicate dishes and vases, like our finest china. But because the dish or vase was so thin, sometimes, as it dried, it would have a small crack in it. This, of course, made the vase or dish very weak; it would break easily. So it was no good. But an unscrupulous merchant would still try to sell it. What he would do is, before he glazed the dish, he would take a very light wax, and he would fill in and cover over the crack. Then with the glaze over it, you couldn't tell the crack was there.

You couldn't tell it was there unless you took the dish outside and held it up against the sun. Then with the light shining behind it, you could tell if there was wax in it or not. You could tell if it was pure, without wax.

The first reason why it's important to choose what is best is so that others won't look at us and say we acted incorrectly or that we did the wrong thing. They'll know we acted with integrity and sincerity toward them.

Second, it's important to choose what is best so that we ourselves will know that we've pleased God in every way and that we've acted as God would have us act. As we choose what is best, we find ourselves "filled with the fruit of righteousness that comes through Jesus Christ—to the glory and praise of God" (Phil. 1:11). We will sense we are acting righteously and that all the godly qualities that Christ wants to produce are taking root in us.

When faced with a decision where there are all kinds of factors, different options, and conflicting possibilities, we want to choose the best course of action. Why? So that no one else will feel that we have acted incorrectly and so that we ourselves will feel that we have pleased God in the matter.

Now, what will make it possible for us to do that—to make the best choice? When we are faced with difficult issues and situations that come up, what will enable us to discern the best course of action and therefore become pure and blameless toward others and righteous in the eyes of God?

The answer is: The more love we have, the better choices we will make and the better people we will become. As our love for each other grows, we will find ourselves making the best choices and becoming a worthy people.

This is what Paul says beginning in verse 9—a growing love will enable us to choose what is best:

> And this is my prayer: that your love may abound more and more in knowledge and depth of insight, so that you may be able to discern what is best and may be pure and blameless for the day of Christ, filled with the fruit of righteousness. (1:9–11a)

As our love for each other grows—a love guided by our *knowledge* of what the Word of God says and guided by our *insight* into the situation—as our love grows, along with our understanding of what the Scripture says and an understanding of what is happening in the situation—we will find ourselves discerning and choosing what is best in a pure and godly way.

When Paul writes that he wants their love to "abound more and more," he doesn't mean abound like a deer or a gazelle. He means *abound* or flow over, like a carbonated drink. His prayer is that their love will just keep on growing and spreading and overflowing toward each other. Because when that abounding kind of love is guided by *knowledge* of what the Word of God says and by *insight* into the situation, we will be able to choose what is best.

Our overflowing love must first of all be guided by *knowledge*—by Scripture. What does the Bible teach about the situation? We don't want a soft, mushy heart to rule our head. Nothing is more harmful than a weak, easy nature that is willing to tolerate anything and overlook any behavior.

"Oh, you're divorcing your wife, leaving your kids, and going off to Mexico with someone from the office. I imagine this must be a difficult time for you. Is there anything I can do to help? Do you need a ride to the airport?"

"Oh, honey child, no wonder you're too tired to go to school. What do you expect when you stay up till 3:00 a.m. playing computer games? But look, why don't you sleep a few more hours, and I'll get you up around 11:00 and take you to school after that."

No, love is not blind. Love sees 20–20. Love is guided by knowledge. The Word of God clearly lets us know the right time to love and the right way to love.

"Yes, I know he wants to be an elder in the church. But he still has a way to go in controlling his anger. Sometimes, when people disagree with him, he tears into them publicly and humiliates them in front of others. I'm afraid he'd be divisive and argumentative in the Board meetings and damage the church. I'd love to see him be an elder someday, but I don't think it would be good for the church right now. The Bible says in 1 Timothy that an elder must be self-controlled, gentle, not quarrelsome. Let's just give him a chance to grow toward that for another couple of years." Our love must be guided by knowledge.

And it must be guided by *insight*, by an understanding of the person and the situation. If a young couple is struggling with infertility, we might not tell too many stories about how cute our kids are. If a friend just lost a job, we might realize that's not the time to openly celebrate the raise or promotion we just got. If a child is not good at athletics, we won't force the issue of going out for school sports.

When our love is guided by knowledge and insight, we will be led to the right choice. We will choose what is best in any situation.

And so I get the phone call: "Pastor, you don't know me, but I've heard about you and your church. My fiancée and I want to get married. Would you perform the ceremony for us?" What is my knowledge of God's Word? Assuming that neither one of them is a genuine believer in Jesus Christ, I could marry them. The Bible tells me that I can't marry a believer to an unbeliever; the Bible says that would be an unequal yoking. But I can marry two unbelievers to each other. My knowledge of the Bible says I could do it. But should I?

What insight do I have in the situation? If I invest the hours in them, will they become part of the church after the ceremony is over? My experience—when I've attempted to do this several times in the past, spending the hours counseling and rehearsing and marrying—is that I never see them again after the wedding. They never really wanted a continuing relationship with me. They just wanted me to give some kind of a halo, or spiritual veneer, to their wedding, kind of like a good luck charm. They just wanted to use me so they could have some vague feeling that they'd gotten married the right way.

But they never did take God seriously, and I never became a significant factor in their lives. My judgment or insight is that the hours it would take should really be put to more profitable use.

"Pastor, will you marry us?"

"Paul, you know, I'd love to get to know you and maybe marry you someday. But when I marry someone, I like to feel like I'm going to be part of their life from then on. I'd love to have that happen with you. Maybe if you and your fiancée could attend the church fairly regularly, and if we could get to know each other over the next six to eight months so that I can see we're going to be part of each other's lives, then I think down the line it would be a lot of fun to marry you."

I love them, but I also love the students at the seminary and the people at the church. My love, guided by knowledge and by insight, leads me to choose what is best—"Paul, come for a while, and when I know that the hours I put in will carry into the future, I'll marry you."

In the Mexican restaurant, the wedding toast is ending. The margaritas are being lifted. I need to make a choice. I need to make the best choice. I love Gary and Joanne. I also love the other people in the church who think it's a sin to drink.

I know what the Word of God says. It doesn't say, "Don't drink." It says, "Don't get drunk." My knowledge says, "There's nothing essentially wrong in toasting with a margarita."

What insight might God give? If I offend those in the church who think it's wrong, they'll get mad at me, and maybe they'll leave the church. But it won't affect their spiritual lives; it'll just affect how they feel about me. But if I wound Gary or Joanne, they could feel ashamed in front of others. And they'll wonder if the pastor and church will forever look down on them.

I love them, and my knowledge of the Word of God and my insight into the situation means that I lift the margarita and join in the toast: "Hear, hear!"

The more love we have, the better choices we will make and the better people we will become—pure and blameless—to the glory of God.

3

IT'S ALL ABOUT YOU, LORD

Philippians 1:12–18

A poet once complained to a friend, "Life's not fair. A banker can write a bad poem, and nobody says anything about it. But if a poet writes a bad check, everybody gets upset."

Former President Jimmy Carter once famously responded to a reporter who was complaining about something with the simple statement: "Life's not fair."

There are times when we feel that way. Something happens to us, and we say, "This isn't fair. Why is this happening to me?"

We seem to be stuck in the same job. Other people get promotions or leave for better jobs in other companies. We work hard, do good work, and get along with people, but for some reason, others who were hired after us seem to advance, and we don't. And we think, "This isn't fair. Why is this happening to me?"

We've finished college. Gotten a graduate degree. We even have a pretty good job. We're kind of ready to settle down, get married. Lots of our friends are getting engaged. We've been going to quite a few weddings lately. But nothing's happening with us. "Lord, where's the person you have for me? I think I have a lot to offer someone. I thought for a while that something might develop with a particular person, but after a few months, it petered out. My married friends are buying condos, going on vacations together. I'm living at home, still going on vacations with my parents. Why, Lord? It doesn't seem fair."

We have difficulty conceiving a child. Other people get married and seem to have one child after another with no difficulty. We long to decorate the nursery, choose the name, shop for baby clothes and toys like other families do. We know that we would be good parents. And we think, "This isn't fair. Why is this happening to me?"

There was a time when the apostle Paul thought back over the past several years of what had taken place in his life. And as he looked at what had happened to him, he certainly could have been tempted to say, "This isn't fair. Why is this happening to me?"

Five years earlier he was worshipping with friends in the temple in Jerusalem. Some Jews, who hated him, saw him there with his friends and started a rumor that one of the friends was a Gentile—that Paul had brought a forbidden, detested Gentile into the sacred Jewish temple.

The rumor spread outside the temple and into the city. People believed it and got agitated and upset. Some hotheads decided to do something about it. They instigated a mob and rushed into the temple. They dragged Paul out of the sanctuary and began to beat him in the courtyard. They intended to beat him to death.

The Roman commander who was responsible for keeping order in the city heard about the riot and rushed to the courtyard with some soldiers, getting there just in time to rescue a bloody Paul. He assumed Paul had wrongfully done something to inflame the crowd. So he arrested him on the spot. He then tried to find out from the crowd, "What's the problem here?"

Some shouted one thing; others shouted something different. The commander realized he wasn't going to get a clear answer. So he took Paul into the prison barracks (Acts 21:27–34).

He decided he'd have one of his men interrogate the prisoner to find out what he'd done. The usual method of interrogation was to tie the prisoner's arms between two posts and give him a bit of the whip until his tongue loosened and he told you what you wanted to know.

But as they were stretching Paul's arms out, Paul looked at the soldier in charge and said, "Is it legal for you to flog a Roman citizen who hasn't been found guilty of anything?" Paul knew it wasn't legal. If a man had Roman citizenship, he was protected from such abuse. If they flogged him without a trial and a verdict, they would all be court-martialed and put in prison themselves. The soldier in charge turned white, told the others to stop right away, and ran to the commander: "This guy's a Roman citizen."

The commander, too, was now worried. He'd arrested a Roman citizen without any real charge or evidence against him. He needed to get a specific charge if he was going to protect his own career. So the next day he gathered the Jewish leaders of the city and brought Paul into the room. "What's the problem you have with this man?" Again, they couldn't agree among themselves. In fact, they started to argue with each other as to what Paul was guilty of. The commander got frustrated, sent them away, and put Paul back in the barracks (Acts 22:24–23:10).

That night the commander got word that some of the Jews had a secret plot to kill Paul. Forty men had taken a vow—they wouldn't eat or drink until they'd killed him. Their plan was for the Jewish leaders to request another meeting with the commander the next day on the pretext that they finally had the information he wanted. And then, as Paul was being transported to the meeting, they would kill him.

The commander realized the situation was too explosive for him to handle. And so, in the dead of night, he bundled Paul off, protected by five hundred men, to the coastal city of Caesarea, about fifty miles to the north. Caesarea was where his boss was headquartered, the Roman governor Felix, who had charge of the whole province.

The commander sent along an explanatory letter to the Roman Governor:

> To his Excellency, Governor Felix. Greetings. This man was about to be killed by the Jews when I rescued him. He's a Roman citizen. When I attempted to find out the problem, all I could get was a lot of religious talk. They didn't seem to have any real criminal charge against him that would merit punishment or death. When I found out they intended to kill him anyway, I thought it best to send him to you. And I've ordered his accusers to present their case to you.

Several days later the accusers arrived in Caesarea. More meetings, this time before Felix. Again, nothing conclusive. But during the proceedings,

Felix began to realize that Paul was not an ordinary Roman citizen. He defended himself well against the accusations. And he seemed to have a lot of friends on the outside. Felix began to think maybe some of these friends would be willing to pay some money—sort of grease the wheels to get Paul released. And so he kept Paul in custody for two years, hoping there was a bribe in it somewhere for him. Paul had done nothing wrong, but for two years he was kept in custody because of some corrupt official (Acts 23:12–24:26).

And the thought could have occurred to Paul, "This isn't fair. Why is this happening to me?"

But it wasn't over yet. After two years in custody, a new governor came to replace Felix. The new governor no sooner took up residence when the Jewish leaders tried again. They appeared in force before him, this time agreeing on some criminal charges against Paul that they hoped would stick. But they couldn't offer any proof of their charges. The new governor thought that perhaps if he set up a trial in the city of Jerusalem, where the events happened, he would be closer to the scene and maybe get better witnesses and more solid evidence. So he asked Paul, "Are you willing to go to Jerusalem, where we can settle this thing once and for all?"

Paul thought, "If I go back to Jerusalem, I'll never make it out alive. They'll find a way to kill me." So he played the last card available to him as a Roman citizen—he appealed to Caesar. He claimed his right as a Roman citizen to have his case put before Caesar himself, kind of like putting it before the Supreme Court. The governor had no choice but to honor his appeal (Acts 24:26–25:12).

But Paul's troubles were still not over. Within a few months, he and some other prisoners were put on a ship and sent off to Rome. Several days out, rough weather hit and slowed their progress. For days, the wind was against them, and they made no headway at all. By that time they were getting near the start of the winter season, when sailing is dangerous and inadvisable. Paul had a sense from the Lord that if they kept going, it was going to be disaster. He urged them to put into the nearest harbor and wait for spring. But the three men in charge of the ship didn't want to do that. The owner of the ship wanted to get his merchandise to Rome and take his profit.

The Roman commander wanted to turn his prisoners over to Rome and be rid of the responsibility. And the pilot of the ship, suddenly seeing that they had a few hours of a gentle breeze, agreed that it was safe to continue (Acts 27:1–13).

After a couple more days at sea, that gentle breeze turned into a hurricane, and now the ship was absolutely helpless against its force. Driven without control, the ship crashed into rocks near an island and broke apart. The soldiers wanted to kill all the prisoners so that none of them could swim away and escape. The commander, however, thinking of Paul, stopped them. Instead, the commander ordered those who could swim to head for the island and those who couldn't to grab a plank or some other piece of the ship so that hopefully the tide would push them to shore.

Amazingly, everyone made it, and they spent the winter on the island. When spring came, another ship took them to Rome. When they got to Rome, Paul had still not been officially charged with anything, so the government allowed him to rent a small house where he could stay. But he had to be chained to a guard 24/7 to make sure he didn't disappear until his case came before Caesar (Acts 27:14–28:16).

The Roman courts moved slowly, and again two years went by while Paul was in house arrest in Rome. He was able to receive visitors in the house, but the chains never left his wrist. Every six hours a new Roman guard took the other end of the chain from the previous guard and put it on his wrist. Paul couldn't move unless the guard moved with him. When he slept, he had to arrange himself so that the chains didn't get under his head or his body. And even though he had no source of income, he still had to pay the rent on the house or else he would be put in some dungeon.

Two years! And the future was still very uncertain. He wasn't sure what would happen if and when he finally did get in front of Caesar. Nero could be crazy at times. Nero might listen to the Jewish accusations and figure, "Hey, if one man's death will make them happy and keep peace in that volatile country, no big deal." Paul knew Jerusalem would have been the end of him, but for all he knew, the same thing could happen in Rome too.

And the thought could have occurred to him, "This isn't fair. Why is this happening to me?"

But that wasn't the thought that occured to him. During the two years of house arrest in Rome, a totally different thought had come into his mind, a thought which brought a big grin to his face and just plain made him happy.

And he wanted to tell some of his friends about it—some dear friends, from a small church in the city of Philippi, who had just sent him some money so that he could afford the rent on the house.

He wanted to thank them for their latest gift. But he also wanted to tell them how he felt about what had been happening to him. As he looked over the past five years of his life—with its mob beating, the unjust imprisonment, the shipwreck, and now the round-the-clock chains—his concern was not "Is it fair?" but "Is it accomplishing anything for God? Is what's happening to me being useful to God in some way? Is it furthering his purposes in the world?"

And so he writes to them, "I want you to know what has happened to me. And because of what's happened, I rejoice."

Now I want you to know, brothers and sisters, that what has happened to me has actually served to advance the gospel. (1:12)

"Contrary to what you'd expect," he says, "my being in prison hasn't hurt the gospel; it's actually helped it to progress. What's happened to me has really accomplished something for God."

He goes on to explain that what has happened to him has really served to advance the gospel in two ways.

First, influential people are being won to the Lord—significant people, powerful people, people who in the future can have a great impact for God. Because of what's happened to him, they're coming to faith in Christ. And to Paul, that's what matters.

In his case, the significant people who are coming to faith are the palace guards who are chained to him 24/7.

Now I want you to know, brothers and sisters, that what has happened to me has actually served to advance the gospel. As a result, it has become clear throughout the whole palace guard and to everyone else that I am in chains for Christ. (1:12–13)

The whole palace guard, he says, is learning about Christ. The palace guard was a very specialized, handpicked military group. They were Caesar's personal bodyguards—strong, courageous, brilliant, sophisticated young men—kind of a mixture of West Point and the Secret Service. They served in the palace guard for twelve years, protecting Caesar and guarding the prisoners that had appealed to him. After twelve years, they transitioned into other influential careers either in the military or government or business. Some went on to be commanding generals of large forces. Others went into public office and became senators or ambassadors to other countries. Still others advanced into the top echelons of business and industry. As a group, they were the movers and shakers of the future, the opinion leaders and kingmakers of the next generation. They were a powerful and strategic group of young men. If you wanted to influence the Roman Empire, you couldn't pick a better group to start with.

And every day for two years one of them had to put on the other end of his chain and for six hours stay within four feet of Paul. Paul had to stifle a grin—he wasn't chained to them; they were chained to him!

During the early months, the guards assumed Paul was like any other prisoner—guilty of some crime like leading a political revolt, embezzling huge sums of money, or illegally profiteering from some disaster. But as they got to know him—when you're chained to somebody for six hours, you've got to talk about something—and listened in on his conversations when his friends visited, none of these seemed to be the accusations against him. Instead, it soon became clear that he was in chains because of someone called Christ. And over the months, as their rotations kept coming around and they put on the chain, Paul would talk with them about Christ.

"Markus, good to see you again. It's been several days. How's Claudia? Last time, you were concerned—she was running a fever for two weeks, getting weaker, and the doctors didn't know why. You were worried. I prayed for her, Markus. I asked God to heal her. How is she? . . . Oh, good, good! I'm glad. I'm glad for you! . . . Oh, you're welcome, you're welcome. . . . Markus, I think God especially has you in mind. Remember last time you asked me why the death of Christ was so important to me? Well, I got to thinking. You know, sometimes, when you're not with me, you're part of

Caesar's bodyguard out in public, right? Well, suppose at some public event you're standing behind Caesar, and an assassin sneaks up behind you with a knife. He's going to swiftly stab you in the back and then get at Caesar. But just before he strikes, another bodyguard, your friend Lysias, sees what's about to happen and quickly tries to intercept. And although Lysias gets in front of the attacker, he's enough off balance that he can't stop the thrust of the knife, and it goes into his heart instead of your back. His death would be important to you, wouldn't it, Markus? It would matter greatly to you because his death would have saved your life. Markus, that's kind of how it is with Christ—his death has saved our lives, forever."

And so it would go, guard after guard chained to Paul, guard after guard hearing about Christ, guard after guard talking to other guards about the prisoner who seemed to be in love with Christ. What happened to Paul— his chains for Christ rippling through the whole palace guard—you could call it a chain reaction.

That's what Paul saw. Because of what had happened to him, people were being won to the Lord—people who in the future could have a great impact for God. And that mattered more to Paul than his personal convenience or the fairness of his situation.

Is it possible that what happens to us—which seems unfair—might be God's way of really accomplishing something for himself?

You feel like you're unjustly stuck in the same job, unable to change or get promoted. Is it possible the reason has nothing to do with your competence or your ability to do other things? Could the reason be because you're developing a friendship with one of your coworkers? And you occasionally have conversations with her about spiritual things. And one week, without your knowing it, as a result of those conversations, she goes with her husband and kids to a large evangelical church. They hear the pastor talk about a project in Africa that the church is committed to next summer, and they decide to go as a family. During that month in Africa, one of the kids discovers the power and reality of God for the first time in his life, and he's forever changed. Twenty years later that kid is back in Africa, part of an evangelistic mission, winning thousands of people to the Lord each year.

And what happened to you, going nowhere at your job, actually served to advance the gospel.

You're not married, so you go on a week's vacation with your parents. That's okay—you get along with them. But you've still got some vacation time left. What to do with it? You hear that a Christian camp is looking for counselors for the high school week. Why not? And up there you have a conversation with a teen who's sensing God's call on his life. Something clicks with him. From then on, he's committed to Christ. When he finishes college, he's in on the ground floor of a tech startup. The company grows, he becomes VP of Development, and his stock is worth millions. Forty percent of his salary goes to the Lord's work, and he's helped God's grace to show through the whole company—day care on the grounds for single parents; six-months' maternity leave for moms and two weeks' leave for dads to help out until things settle down; eight percent company matching of retirement benefits. And everything about his life has the fragrance of the Lord. What happened to you as a result of your singleness actually served to advance the Lord's work.

Your difficulty in conceiving a child leads you to foster care. Over a period of years, scores of children come through your home. Each one learns about Christ. And as they grow and marry, each one establishes a Christian home; each one raises kids to know Christ, kids who will do the same when they grow up. You begin a multiplying chain reaction into generations to come. And what happened to you, your infertility, actually served to advance the gospel.

And so we say with Paul, "The question is not 'Is what's happening to me fair?' but instead, 'Is what's happening to me accomplishing something for God? Is what's happening to me being useful to God in some way? Is it furthering his purposes in the world?'" And when we see that it is, we say, "It's all about you, Lord. It's not about me. It's all about you."

That's the first thing Paul has in mind when he writes, "what has happened to me has actually served to advance the gospel." He sees that people are being won to the Lord—people who in the future can have a great impact for God.

Paul sees a second way that his circumstances served to advance the gospel: other pastors in Rome were preaching more boldly than ever before. Not only were people being won to the Lord, but other pastors were speaking out with greater confidence, stepping out more courageously in their own ministries.

And because of my chains, most of the brothers and sisters have become confident in the Lord and dare all the more to proclaim the gospel without fear. (1:14)

As other pastors in Rome saw Paul's courage and heard the reports about his impact on the palace guard and how significant people were responding to the gospel, it led them to speak out more boldly and fearlessly, to hold more public meetings, and to take a stand for godliness. So again, what had happened to Paul was actually serving to advance the gospel.

Unfortunately, some of these other pastors had mixed motives in what they were doing. Not all of them, of course. Many of them had nothing but pure motives as they preached. But there were others—they kind of hoped their preaching would stick it to Paul a bit. Oh, they were preaching a good message. Of course they wanted people to accept Christ. But at the same time they kind of wanted to rub it in Paul's face.

Their problem was that Paul was getting too much attention. As far as they were concerned, he was just a little bit too famous. Big shot apostle comes to town as an imperial prisoner, guarded by Caesar's personal bodyguards. All the Christians in Rome were talking about him and singing his praises. Some of the local pastors got a bit jealous of all the attention Paul was getting. Their noses got out of joint. Who was he to come into their city and get all the praise after they'd been there for years? So some of them took advantage of the situation to ratchet things up a bit so they, too, would become more prominent and more famous. It was kind of a rivalry with them. Their ambition was to be as noticed and esteemed as Paul. And they secretly hoped that as the attention shifted to them, the big "star" would get his comeuppance. Then he could see what it was like to have someone else praised while he was stuck in chains. "He'll see us out there growing big churches, holding big rallies, getting a lot of press, while he can't go four feet without hitting the end of the chain."

Paul knew this was going on:

> And because of my chains, most of the brothers and sisters have become confident in the Lord and dare all the more to proclaim the gospel without fear.
>
> It is true that some preach Christ out of envy and rivalry, but others out of goodwill. The latter do so out of love, knowing that I am put here for the defense of the gospel. The former preach Christ out of selfish ambition, not sincerely, supposing that they can stir up trouble for me while I am in chains. But what does it matter? The important thing is that in every way, whether from false motives or true, Christ is preached. And because of this I rejoice. (1:14–18)

"The good ones," he says, "mean me well. They have nothing but goodwill toward me. They know that I'm put here for the defense of the gospel, and they want me to see that they've joined me."

When Paul says that he's "put here," he's using a military term—"This is my military assignment; these are my military orders. The good ones know that God has assigned me to these chains and to a courtroom appearance before Caesar—that God has ordered me here to defend the gospel at the highest level in the Roman Empire. They love me, and they want to do their part where they can.

"I'm aware that there are others who have mixed motives. They'd like to agitate me. They feel I should get a little of my own medicine—that I should feel chafing and resentment while they're moving freely about town, adding to their reputations. I know their preaching is partly motivated by envy, rivalry, and ambition.

"But you know what? Christ is being preached! And that's what matters. What's happening to me is actually serving to advance the gospel. And that's more important than my chains and my reputation. That's more important than my convenience or whether life is being fair to me or not. What matters is whether God is accomplishing something for himself."

If you had asked Paul, "Is it fair, what's happened to you?" he would have said, "No." If you had asked him, "Has it been fun? Has it been enjoyable? Is it something you would have chosen for your life?" he would have said, "Of course not." But in the midst of it all, he stopped and asked himself, "Is what's happening to me accomplishing something for God?" And when he saw that the answer was "Yes," that mattered more to him than his personal convenience or the fairness of his situation. What happened to him actually accomplished something for God, and that's what counted.

My friend, God doesn't promise that your circumstances will be fair. But he does promise that there will always be something in them that connects to Christ—something that will serve his purposes. There will always be a word to speak, a kindness to offer, or a prayer to lift up. There will always be something for Christ in your circumstances. Look for it.

What happens to us can serve to advance the gospel. And the joy of life comes when we can honestly say, "It's not about me, Lord. It's all about you. It's only about you."

4

A WIN–WIN SITUATION

Philippians 1:19–26

Every so often we find ourselves in a win–win situation. No matter which way it goes, we come out ahead—we win.

At school you decide to drop your second-period psychology class and instead take a second-period economics class. There are two economic classes that meet second period, and as you think about the two classes, each one has something going for it. "This class has a great teacher who makes the subject really interesting and fun. The other class has my best friend in it and the pretty girl I've been trying to get to know. Either class will be great—a win–win situation."

"This Saturday my boyfriend thinks he can get the day off work, and we can drive up to the mountain orchards and pick some apples. If he can't get the day off work, well, there are three of us girls that have been talking about hitting the mall and doing some serious shopping. The stores are having sales to clear their fall merchandise to make way for the winter season. The mountains with my boyfriend or the mall with my girlfriends—either one is great, a win–win situation."

"My husband has promised a get-away weekend. If it's sunny and doesn't rain, we go up the coast to Carmel. If a storm hits the coast, then we go out to Palm Springs. Three days alone with my husband—Carmel or Palm Springs. Hey, either one is great, win–win."

You get an email from your grown kids. They're trying to decide between spending the money to fly themselves and the grandkids out to California for Thanksgiving or to fly you and your wife to Orlando, where they'll meet you for three days at Disney World. "All right! Three days at Thanksgiving with our kids and grandkids. Less trouble and travel for us if they come to California but more fun and adventure if we go to Florida. Either one is fine, a win–win situation."

Your company has been bought out, and your department is being merged into the same department in the other company. You're waiting to hear how you'll be affected. You've been told that you'll either be given a $250,000 buy-out severance package or you'll be made a vice president in the new, combined company with increased responsibilities and pay. "Two hundred fifty thousand dollars! Man! I could take six months off, laze around, and still have enough to start my own business—that bicycle sales and repair shop that I've always wanted. On the other hand, VP—big challenge, great future. Whichever way they decide is fine with me—a win–win situation."

It's great to be in a win–win situation, where no matter which way it goes, we come out ahead—we win.

The apostle Paul once found himself in that kind of situation—no matter which way it went, he was going to come out ahead. As he explained it in a letter to some friends, "A few months from now, at my trial, Caesar's going to make a decision. He's either going to put me to death or he's going to let me live. Hmmm—man, talk about a win–win situation. Either one would be great!"

And we think, "Waaait a minute! That doesn't sound like a win–win situation. I would think one of those would be highly preferable and the other one would be on the bottom of the list of things I'd want to happen. He's going to be put to death or he's going to be allowed to live—and that's a win–win? How so?"

And Paul would reply, "Because I'm going to get a reward; I'm going to get heaven's praise for doing something at my trial, and then whatever Caesar decides after that will be great either way. I'm going to do something at my trial that's going to bring me God's final stamp of approval, and then whatever Caesar decides after that will be a win–win situation for me."

What is Paul about to do, for which he expects some heavenly reward, some praise? What does he expect to do that will bring him such approval?

And how can Caesar's decision after that be a win–win for him either way? How could he possibly say, "You know, I could live or die, and I'll take either one"? How could we ever get to the point where we could look at such drastically opposite outcomes as that and say, "Hey, either one would be a win–win situation"?

The answers to these questions emerge in a letter Paul was writing to some dear friends. For two years he'd been in house arrest, chained 24/7 to a guard, every six hours to another one of Caesar's personal bodyguards, awaiting a trial on some trumped-up charges. House arrest was better than being dumped in a dungeon because he could have visitors and be fairly comfortable as long as he could come up with the money for food and rent.

Some dear friends from a city about eight hundred miles away had just sent him a significant sum of money to help him stay in the house, and so he was writing to thank them.

He also wanted to let them know that what had happened to him had actually served to advance the gospel in two very significant ways. First, Caesar's bodyguards, who were attached to him 24/7, were being won to the Lord. And second, local pastors in Rome were preaching more boldly than ever before. And Paul's spirit was, "Christ is preached. And because of this I rejoice" (Phil. 1:18).

But he also had a third reason for writing. He was not only grateful for their gift and happy for how things had turned out for the gospel; he was also happy for how things had turned out for himself. "I have another reason for rejoicing because what's happened is also going to bring me some great reward. In addition to advancing the gospel, my circumstances are also going to bring me some divine approval and praise."

This is what he means when he says at the end of verse 18 and into verse 19:

> *Yes, and I will continue to rejoice, for I know that through your prayers and God's provision of the Spirit of Jesus Christ what has happened to me will turn out for my deliverance.*

When he says this "will turn out for my deliverance," the word *deliverance* is the word for "salvation" in his language. Paul is saying, "What's happened to me is leading toward that great day in heaven when my salvation will be complete, when I will get God's final stamp of approval—heaven's praise and reward."

It's helpful to remember that the Bible uses the word *salvation* or *deliverance* in three senses. We have a past salvation, a present salvation, and a future salvation.

The Bible talks about our past salvation—when we believed that Jesus died for our sins and we trusted his death as payment of our punishment. We were delivered forever from hell and given eternal life.

The Bible talks about our present salvation—how we're being saved now from the power of sin; how we're being protected from the hatred of Satan; how we're being delivered from a life of misery and emptiness and futility; how we instead find ourselves living joyfully, confidently, and expectantly.

And then the Bible talks about our future salvation—when we're with the Lord: delivered from pain and sorrow; in the presence of our Savior; smiling, loving, and celebrating.

Paul is looking at that future day when God will reward him and bless him and give the final stamp of approval to his life. When he says, "What's happened to me will turn out for my deliverance or salvation," he means, "this will contribute greatly to my reward and praise in heaven."

So Paul is rejoicing because he sees he's going to be rewarded in heaven for something he's about to do, and whatever Caesar chooses to do after that will be a win–win situation either way.

Now, what is Paul about to do that will bring him this great reward? What does he see happening in the next few months that's going to result in heaven's approval?

He's going to have a chance to exalt Christ like never before to the whole world. He's going to have an unbelievable opportunity to magnify Christ, to display him large to the Roman Empire, and to honor him before the whole world:

> *I eagerly expect and hope that I will in no way be ashamed, but will have sufficient courage so that now as always Christ will be exalted in my body, whether by life or by death.* (1:20)

Christ is going to be exalted, Christ is going to be lifted up, and Christ is going to be displayed. Paul is going to present Christ to the highest court of the whole Roman world. And his expectation, he adds, is that when the time comes he's going to come through with flying colors. "I'm not going to wimp out, I don't expect to come out of there beaten down, bested, feeling like a loser, or ashamed. Nope."

> *Through your prayers and God's provision of the Spirit of Jesus Christ. . . . I eagerly expect and hope that I will in no way be ashamed, but will have sufficient courage so that now as always Christ will be exalted in my body. (1:19–20a)*

Paul is eagerly anticipating his opportunity to magnify Christ in Caesar's court. He's not like someone who carries a snapshot in his wallet, and if you ask to see it, he'll show it to you. "Oh, you want to know about Christ. Yeah, I think I have a picture of him somewhere. Let me see. Yeah, here it is. Sorry, it's kind of small and a little bit old."

No, Paul has an enlarged, life-sized, full-length poster board picture that he carries all the time. You can hardly see Paul behind it. His whole life is Christ. Christ died for him. Christ chose him. Christ freed him from his past. Christ called him to an eternal future. Christ is his perfect model. Christ is his passion. Christ is his Lord.

And now he has a chance to exalt Christ and to display him to the whole world, which will climax his reward in heaven.

And after Paul exalts Christ to the world, Caesar can make whatever decision he wants. After Paul displays Christ to the world, then whatever happens to his body either way is fine. Whether the trial leads to life or death, no matter, it's a win–win situation. If Caesar releases him, he'll go on serving Christ. If Caesar puts him to death, he'll finally get to be with the Christ he loves. He's in a win–win situation:

> *I eagerly expect and hope that I will in no way be ashamed, but will have sufficient courage so that now as always Christ will be exalted in my body, whether by life or by death.* [Whether it leads to life or to

death, whether I am released or sentenced. Either way is fine.] *For to me, to live is Christ and to die is gain.* (1:20–21)

"I come out ahead either way. If I live, I serve Christ longer. If I die, I bow before him and adore him forever."

It was such a win–win situation for Paul that if you asked him which one he'd pick, he'd have a hard time making up his mind. They were both so good he wouldn't know which one to choose. If you asked him to decide, he'd be torn between the two, pulled in both directions:

For to me, to live is Christ and to die is gain. If I am to go on living in the body, this will mean fruitful labor for me. Yet what shall I choose? I do not know! I am torn between the two: I desire to depart and be with Christ, which is better by far; but it is more necessary for you that I remain in the body. Convinced of this [that it's more beneficial for you], *I know that I will remain, and I will continue with all of you for your progress and joy in the faith, so that through my being with you again your boasting in Christ Jesus will abound on account of me.* (1:21–26)

If you gave Paul his druthers, he'd probably pick going to be with Christ. Man, what could be better than that? Nothing! On the other hand, what would serve God's purposes more? Probably staying here and being available to the churches a bit longer. And as Paul thought about it, he was pretty sure that was what God was going to decide, which meant Caesar would release him and he would visit his dear friends again.

We look at Paul, and we think, "How in the world do you get to the point he was at—where you're as happy to die and be with Christ as you are to stay here on earth and serve his purposes? How do you get to that point? 'To live, Christ! To die, better yet!'"

We're not there. I'm not there. There have been a couple of times when I sensed a teensy bit of it. But I was still a long way from it.

One time, when I was in college, I was driving my Volkswagon Beetle home from church on a Sunday. I was on the Pasadena Freeway, going from Los Angeles to Pasadena. The Pasadena Freeway is the oldest freeway in the state—three lanes, very narrow, and a curving, winding road. It was the first rain of the season, which meant that the roads were pretty slick. I was in the outside lane, doing about fifty around a long curve near the Chinatown area. Cars were solid in the center lane to my left, and there was a wall or fence to my right. As I came around the curve, I suddenly saw that the car ahead of me had spun out and was sideways in my lane about thirty yards ahead of me. I immediately jammed on the brakes, but because of the slickness of the road and the lightness of the VW, the little car started hydroplaning—and I was sliding at forty or fifty miles an hour into the side of the car in front of me. Like all VW Beetles in those days, the engine was in the back and just a thin, empty trunk space was in front. As I helplessly gripped the wheel and headed into the crash, the thought flashed through my mind, "Lord, I'm coming home." That was it—"Lord, I'm coming home." I hit hard, snapped the steering wheel, and banged my head against the windshield. But when it was all over, I was uninjured.

As I later reflected on the thought that had flashed through my mind—"Lord, I'm coming home"—I was kind of happy about that. It seemed to show a deep internal confidence that if I died, I was going to heaven. Without having had a chance to think about it, the thought was just spontaneously there: "When I die, I'm with the Lord." I was pleased to sense that within me.

But you know, I was also glad that I didn't die. I still wasn't anywhere near where Paul was—"either one is fine." No, no—"Lord, I'm glad to know I'm coming home someday, but I'm in no hurry. No rush. I'd kinda like to stay down here for a while. For me, 'to live' is to get engaged, marry, raise a family, and do some things on earth. 'To die,' well, it's nice to know that there's nothing to fear because it's all taken care of, but let's leave that out there in the future for a while longer." I was still a long way from "To live—to serve Christ; to die—better yet, to gain Christ!"

I was kind of like the story of three friends who arrive at the Pearly Gates at the same time. As Peter shows them around heaven, he asks what kind of comments or remarks they'd most like to hear from their family and friends at their funerals that were about to take place.

One man says, "I'd like to hear them say I was a great doctor and a good family man." The second man says, "I'd like to hear that I was a wonderful husband and that during my career as a school teacher I made a difference in many lives." The third man says, "Those both sound great, but what I'd really like to hear them say is, 'Hey, look, he's moving.'"

That's kind of where I was after the accident: "Hey, look, I'm still down here and moving. Good!"

I got a little closer to where Paul was some years later. By then Nell and I were married. We had five small children, ages two to twelve, and were living in Dallas. One night about two in the morning I woke up with a terrible pain in my chest, which seemed to be radiating down my left side and arm. I ruled out heartburn or indigestion, for I'd never had any of that. I knew enough about heart attacks to know that they started in your chest and went down your left side. And I thought, "If I'm having a heart attack, I could be dead within a few minutes." The thought went through my head, "Lord, I'm ready to come, but it seems like a dirty trick to play on Nell and the kids." I waited a few more minutes. The pain didn't get any worse, but it was still troubling, so I woke Nell and explained to her what was happening. We called a friend to come and stay with the kids, and we went to the emergency room. After several hours, the pain went away, and the doctors never did figure out what caused it.

As I later thought about what flashed through my mind—"Lord, I'm ready to come, I'm ready to come, but it seems like a dirty trick to play on Nell and the kids"—I was a little bit closer to where Paul was—"Lord, I'm happy to come, but I think it would really be better for others if I remained here a bit longer."

But it still wasn't "Lord, if you give me my choice, I actually want to come. But if you think others need me here, I guess I could stay."

How did Paul get to the point where he saw it as nothing but a win–win situation? Where, if he actually had his choice, he'd rather be with Christ? How did he get there?

I think first he had a clearer picture of what death is, and that made him more willing for it to happen. He saw what death really means for a Christian, and of course it was great.

For Paul, death was simply a departure—"I am torn between the two: I desire to depart and be with Christ, which is better by far" (1:23). The word *depart* was a word used in his language for breaking up camp and heading home. Breaking up camp—I've been out in the boonies long enough. "Enough of mosquitoes, enough of cold showers, enough of bears poking around the food at night, enough of freezing nights. Let's pack this stuff up and head home, where it will be so much better. Heading home!"

The word *depart* was also used for loosening the lines that held a ship to the pier and letting the ship sail. Since we don't sail much, imagine you've been traveling overseas for two weeks, and it's time to come home. You lug all your bags into a foreign airport. For two weeks you've been living out of a suitcase. In one hotel room after another, the rooms are small and cramped, the chairs aren't comfortable, and the pillows don't feel right. The heating or AC broke down in your room one night, but you couldn't explain it to the night clerk because he didn't speak English. You can't read the street signs because they're in a different language. You're worried about using the subway because you're not sure you've figured it out right. The money is different, and you constantly have to calculate on the spot how much you're paying for things. You're on edge all the time because you're afraid somebody will lift your wallet or steal your passport.

After two weeks, weary and frazzled, you come into the airport and look at the listing of flights. You're searching for your flight home. You find it. "Estimated time of *departure*"—"Delayed." "Oh no!" Worse yet—"Flight Canceled." "Noooo! I want to go home. I want to depart and go home."

That's how Paul saw it. "I want to depart. I want to go home and be with Christ."

If we really understood how good death's going to be, who wouldn't want it? I think that first of all, Paul clearly saw what death means for a Christian—it's going home!

And then secondly, the reason he was at the point where "To live is to serve Christ, to die is to be with Christ" is because Christ was everything to him. Christ was his life. Christ was his eternity. Christ was his passion.

And when Christ is everything, whether you serve him or see him, it's a win–win situation.

5

WHERE'S THE GIFT RECEIPT?

Philippians 1:27–30

During 2003 the United States was intent on two things: rebuilding Iraq following the overthrow of Saddam Hussein and capturing Osama bin-Laden, the terrorist responsible for bombing the Twin Towers in New York City.

Let's suppose that during this time there was a small town on the edge of Iraq, near the Saudi border. Let's call the town Bajuk. It's off by itself, a small community, and no other towns are around for thirty to forty miles.

Let's suppose this Iraqi town on the Saudi border unexpectedly captures Osama bin-Laden as he tries to slip into his Saudi homeland. The town leaders of Bajuk immediately contact our Commanding General in Iraq—"Come and get Osama bin-Laden." He does, and before long, Osama bin-Laden is taken into custody to await trial.

Our government is extremely grateful to this town. The president makes a trip to meet with the town elders and rewards them with improvements to their community—roads, schools, electricity, air-conditioning. Some of their brightest young men and women are brought to the United States for education in our finest universities. One of them gets a Ph.D. in geology, returns to his hometown of Bajuk, and soon after discovers the largest pool of underground oil on the planet. Nobody knew it was there, but there's a vast subterranean lake of oil dwarfing any other known source of oil in the world.

The town leaders again contact the United States. "How would the United States like to enter into a direct and exclusive agreement with Bajuk to have sole access to all this oil at bargain prices? We'll sell it only to you for just half the world-market price." And suddenly there's the possibility that the price of gas will drop to forty cents a gallon and that all of our energy needs will be met forever!

But is Bajuk's offer legal? The president consults with his legal experts. "Can Bajuk do this? Can Bajuk deal with us directly? We're in the process of setting up a government in Iraq. Won't the national government of Iraq control the oil rights in the country?"

The legal experts research the issue and come back. "Mr. President, the new Constitution of Iraq is not in place yet. Nothing's official. Things are still fluid. It would be possible for Bajuk to secede from Iraq, declare itself an independent country, and be free to do whatever it wants. If we move quickly, Mr. President, it could be legally done."

"But could we make it stick?" says the president. "Bajuk's a small, isolated community. If it becomes an independent country, it'll have no military defenses. Its larger neighbors could easily overrun it and absorb it into one of their countries, and we'd lose everything."

The vice president speaks up. "Mr. President, I have a wild idea. Rather than have them declare themselves an independent state, let's offer to make them the fifty-first state of the United States of America. They're a long way off, but so is Alaska, so is Hawaii. If we vote them into the Union as the state of Bajuk, zip code 99999, we can then deal with them as one of our states. We can permanently station troops there, we can build all the pipelines and refineries we need, and we can make sure things are environmentally safe. We can do anything we want because they'd belong to us."

"Intriguing idea, Tom. Does that mean they'd be citizens of the United States?"

"Yes, it would, Mr. President. They'd be citizens of the United States. They'd elect senators and representatives; they'd get Social Security; they could come to the mainland any time they wanted to. Our Bill of Rights would protect them: they'd have freedom of speech, they'd be innocent until proven guilty, and all our laws would apply to them—property, inheritance, voting. They'd be full citizens of the United States.

"We can legally do it, huh? . . . All right, let's ask them!"

So the president makes another trip to Bajuk. "How'd you guys like to be citizens of the United States?" And he explains the plan to them.

Never in their wildest dreams! "Citizens of the United States! Free, full citizens of the richest, most powerful country in the world. How quick can we make it happen?"

And so, three months later, there's a little green sign on the side of the road just before you reach the town of Bajuk: "Welcome to Bajuk, the Fifty-First State of the United States of America, Population: 9,000." And from then on, if you're a resident of Bajuk, you're unique and special in all the region.

The apostle Paul had some friends who lived in a town just like that—a small town off by itself. But if you lived in that small town, it was like living in imperial Rome itself, even though Rome was eight hundred miles away. It was the small town of Philippi, and it had a unique, special status. The sign outside the town said, "Welcome to Philippi, a Colony of Rome."

They were Roman citizens and had been for ninety years. It all happened when they were on the winning side in a battle that was fought on a plain just outside their city limits. It was a battle between Caesar and two of his generals—a civil war. The town of Philippi backed Caesar, and when he won, he showed his gratitude. As a reward, Caesar made them a colony of Rome. Lots of his top military retired there. To live in Philippi was to be a citizen of Rome. You spoke Latin, you wore Roman clothing, you used Roman money, and you followed Roman customs. You were a Roman citizen.

Paul had some friends who lived in that city. They were part of a small church he had helped start. And as Paul writes to them, a small church in a city that prided itself on being Roman citizens, he says to them, "You are citizens of a place vastly more important than Rome."

"You are citizens of heaven. You as a church are a group of citizens, formed not by Caesar but by Christ, loyal not to Rome but to heaven. You are citizens of heaven, placed in the city of Philippi, and Christ is your Lord, your King, your Ruler, your Leader, the one to whom you pledge allegiance. 'I pledge allegiance to Jesus Christ and to the kingdom over which he rules.'"

As Paul writes to his friends about being citizens of heaven, he stresses how this should affect their daily conduct. He talks about how they should live worthy of such citizenship.

And we want to listen carefully to his words, for he is speaking to us too. As Christians in America, we are citizens of the most powerful country on earth. But more than that, we are citizens of heaven, citizens with a King above and a purpose below. We're citizens of heaven, with a Lord on high and a concern on earth. And we want to hear these words from our King about how to be a worthy citizen in his kingdom.

We're going to drop into Paul's letter to the believers at Philippi just after he's finished giving them the news about himself. He's been under house arrest for two years. Surprisingly, he tells them, this hasn't hurt the gospel; in fact, it's actually helped it to advance. Caesar's personal bodyguards are being won to the Lord, young men who will influence the country for decades to come. Local pastors in Rome are preaching more boldly. The gospel is progressing! And Paul is happy.

He's also pretty happy about what all this means to him. In a few months he's going to have a chance to display Christ at the highest levels of Roman government, to exalt Christ before Caesar's court. That's only going to add to his reward in heaven. And after he lifts up Christ at his trial, it doesn't matter much whether Caesar releases him or sentences him to death. It'll be a win–win situation either way. To live—that means he'll serve Christ more. To die—that means he'll see Christ sooner. He expects, however, to live and to come see his dear friends again.

But enough about his circumstances. He wants to talk about their lives and about how they should live worthy of their heavenly citizenship. "I expect to visit you again," he writes, "but whether that happens or not, I at least want to hear that you are living worthily as citizens of heaven":

Whatever happens, conduct yourselves in a manner worthy of the gospel of Christ. Then, whether I come and see you or only hear about you in my absence, I will know that you stand firm in the one Spirit. (1:27a)

When Paul writes "conduct yourselves," he's looking at our heavenly citizenship. In his language, the words *conduct yourselves* mean "live as citizens."

More than citizens of America, we are citizens of heaven. We are to live as citizens, conducting ourselves in a manner worthy of the gospel.

Now, if we're going to live as citizens of heaven, how will that show up? If we're going to live worthy of the gospel, what will that mean?

It means we'll stand for God's truth and not be scared off when someone opposes it. We'll contend for God's truth, and we won't be frightened or intimidated by those that are against it:

> Whatever happens, conduct yourselves in a manner worthy of the gospel of Christ. Then, whether I come and see you or only hear about you in my absence, I will know that you stand firm in the one Spirit, striving together as one for the faith of the gospel without being frightened in any way by those who oppose you. (1:27–28a)

To live worthily as citizens of heaven means we're united in a common resolve to fight for the truth of the gospel. We're committed to pressing for God's truth without being intimidated or scared away by those that are hostile to it. To live worthy of the gospel is to stand for God's truth without shying away or being spooked like a horse when someone comes against us.

It might mean, in high school or college, saying, "Yes, I'm a virgin. And with God's help, I hope to stay one until I'm married. Someone's going to get something special that no one else has ever gotten. Someone's going to know that they're the only one who's ever gotten it and that they can count on it for the rest of their life." And if someone starts to ridicule or make fun, we don't back down. We have a quiet strength. We are citizens of a King, and we know his truth. To live worthy of the gospel is to stand for God's truth and to not be scared off.

It might mean, in business, saying to the corporate bosses, "I don't feel comfortable taking our international clients to night clubs or arranging for 'hostesses' to entertain them in their hotel rooms at night. I don't think we should do business that way." And if someone starts to attack or get angry, to browbeat or intimidate, we don't back down. We are citizens of a King, and we know his truth. And we don't give way. To live worthy of the gospel is to stand for God's truth and to not be scared off.

It might mean, in conversations with relatives or friends, saying, "There aren't many ways to heaven. There's only one. Other religions can't give you eternal life—you must believe in Jesus as your savior from sin. You can't just be a good person and earn your way into heaven—you must believe that it's only by Jesus' death that your sins can be forgiven." And if someone starts to get hostile or to get agitated and say that we're being narrow-minded, we gently and quietly answer, "Truth is narrow; two plus two only equals four. And the only way to be saved from your sin is to believe that Jesus died to pay your penalty for you." To live worthy of the gospel is to stand for God's truth and not be scared off by those against it.

And when we live that way—when we stand for the truth and can't be frightened away from it—some disturbing impression is made on our opponents, and some affirming sense comes to us. When we stand for God's truth, and no amount of ridicule or harassment can get us to back down, no threat of punishment can intimidate us, no fear of loss or litigation can make us change—when we stand for God's truth and cannot be scared off, some foreboding sense comes on those who oppose us, and some assuring confidence comes to us.

The disturbing impression made on our opponents is that they are under God's judgment and heading to destruction. When we stand for God's truth and cannot be scared off, it "is a sign to them that they will be destroyed" (Phil. 1:28).

How is it a sign to them? How is our standing for the truth without being intimidated a sign to them that they are wrong, under God's judgment, and heading to destruction?

This disturbing impression comes on them because deep in their hearts, they know it's not natural for someone to stand against the ridicule or hostility of a group. Deep in their hearts, they know that when a group begins to browbeat and threaten or attack, people cave in. They know the normal human response is that when people see that they're going to be penalized for holding a certain view, they find some way to back off from it.

But when they see us continue to stand without being intimidated, it makes a disturbing impression on them because something unexplainable is happening. They see in us a quiet resolve that they don't have. They see a certainty and strength that can only be explained as coming from somewhere else. And deep in their hearts, a convicting voice says to them, "You know they are right, and unless you change, you'll be under the judgment of the God who is in them."

When you stand for the truth and are not scared off, a disturbing impression is made on those who oppose you—that unless they change, they'll be under the judgment of God.

At the same time, an affirming sense comes to us. When we stand for the truth and cannot be scared off, even though we're ridiculed or harassed, threatened or punished, when we stand for the truth and don't back down even though we suffer for it, some assuring confidence comes to us—that God has genuinely saved us, that we truly belong to him, and that our salvation is certain:

This is a sign to them that they will be destroyed, but that you will be saved—and that by God. (1:28)

When we stand for the truth and cannot be scared off, even though we suffer for it, it's a proof to us that we are genuinely saved and that we truly belong to God.

Why is this the case? Why does our standing firm and suffering for the truth become a proof to us that our salvation is secure?

Because suffering is God's way of identifying those who are his. Suffering is God's way of confirming those who belong to him. Suffering is God's recognition, God's assurance that you are living worthy of heaven's kingdom.

The Bible says that all who desire to live a godly life in Christ Jesus will suffer persecution (2 Tim. 3:12). If you're suffering for righteousness, this indicates that you're living a godly life and that you belong to him.

The Bible says that we'll go through many hardships and tribulations to enter the kingdom (Acts 14:22). So if you're going through hardships and tribulation for the sake of righteousness, it's proof or a confirmation that you're entering the kingdom.

Suffering is God's way of identifying those who are his. Suffering is God's "gift" of assurance that you truly belong to Christ:

For it has been granted to you on behalf of Christ not only to believe in him, but also to suffer for him, since you are going through the same struggle you saw I had, and now hear that I still have. (1:29–30)

When Paul writes, "it has been granted to you," the language he uses means, "it's a gift that has been given to you." And the meaning is that it's a loving, gracious gift, an especially thoughtful gift that proves something wonderful to you—that you belong to him. Suffering is God's gift that tells you, "You are saved."

At first glance, suffering may not seem like a gift we'd want. We'd be tempted to look for the gift receipt so that we can return it. When somebody gives us a gift, they usually say something like, "If you don't want it, or if you want to exchange it, there's a gift receipt in the box."

But God says, "There's no gift receipt. The gift is too important, too special, too significant. It tells you something wonderful—suffering tells you that you're living worthy of my kingdom and that you belong to me." Proudly receive the gift as a sign of honor from God.

You are a citizen of heaven, a citizen with a King above and a purpose below—to stand for God's truth and not be scared off, knowing deep in your heart that you belong to him. Conduct yourself in a manner worthy of the gospel that saved you.

6

IT'S NOT THINKING LESS OF YOURSELF;
IT'S THINKING OF YOURSELF LESS

Philippians 2:1–4

A few years ago one of my seminary students was speaking to the class. He was a Korean-American who had grown up in this country and was active in Korean-American churches. He told the class that the average Korean-American church goes about eight years, and then it splits because of some disagreement or dissension among the members or the leadership.

He mentioned one Korean church where the pastor and the elders were at great odds with each other. The elders met in secret to vote to have the pastor fired. The pastor heard about the meeting and retaliated. He got a petition signed by other members of the church denouncing the elders as disruptive and then got a judge to give a restraining order so that the elders couldn't come within five hundred yards of the church building. Shortly after that the elders started their own church and took almost half the congregation with them.

Apparently the reputation of Korean churches arguing and splitting is fairly well known. One Chinese lady told me half jokingly, "When two Japanese meet, they start a business; when two Chinese meet, they start a restaurant; when two Koreans meet, they start a church."

Now, I don't mean to pick on Korean-American churches. Koreans take their churches seriously. What goes on there matters greatly to them. But when conflict arises, a frequent solution of this ethnic minority is to start another church.

Other evangelical believers have a different solution for conflict or disagreement—instead of starting a new church, they just go to a different church. They pick up their marbles and go elsewhere, like the joke about the lone castaway who was rescued. When his rescuers asked him about two huts they noticed on the desolate island, he pointed to one and said, "That's the church I belong to." "What's the other hut?" "Oh, that's the church I used to belong to."

Fortunately, many churches do stay together. They have their disagreements. They experience conflicts. But they stay together. The members don't start new churches or leave for other churches. The splits and ruptures that happen at some churches don't happen at theirs. Differences of opinion, misunderstandings, and personal slights don't cause an exodus from their church. Why not? What prevents that from happening? What enables some churches to continue in harmony and unity?

One of the early Christian churches was experiencing conflict and disagreement. The culture of their city fostered such a spirit of pride and independence that most individuals expected to have things their way. And as the apostle Paul saw the believers tending in that direction, he appealed to them in a letter to remain unified and like-minded.

He had already spoken to them about the many things that had brought joy to his life—their recent financial gift, his palace guards coming to faith in Christ, local pastors becoming more bold in their preaching, and his own expectation of exalting Christ before Nero. He has lots of reasons for joy. "But if you want to make my joy complete," he says, "if you want me to be completely happy here in prison, let me hear that you're living in harmony with each other. Let me hear that you're like-minded, that your thoughts are focused on matters of ministry, that you're loving each other, and that you're one together in spirit and purpose":

Make my joy complete by being like-minded, having the same love, being one in spirit and of one mind. (2:2)

When Paul talks about "being like-minded," he doesn't mean believers need to have the same opinions or agree on everything. But we should have a common way of approaching a matter. We should come at things with the same attitude—knowing that God has called us to be at peace in our spirit with each other, that there is a larger purpose that he has for us as a church, and that we've committed ourselves to loving each other and living in harmony.

Paul appeals to the Philippian church to bring this joy to his life. "Would you do this for me?" he says. "I know God's made it possible for you to do it. It's in you to do it. Since God's working in your life to make it happen, I know you can do this for me—you can make my joy complete by living in harmony."

> *Therefore if you have any encouragement from being united with Christ, if any comfort from his love, if any common sharing in the Spirit, if any tenderness and compassion, then make my joy complete by being like-minded, having the same love, being one in spirit and of one mind.* (2:1–2)

When he writes *if*—"if you have any encouragement from being united with Christ"—he writes it in such a way that in his language, the implication is "If you have any encouragement from Christ, and I know you do." He's not being uncertain or wondering if it's true. He's assuming that's the case. It would be like my saying, "If it's my birthday—and it is—I get to pick where we go out to eat." I could just as easily say, "Since it's my birthday, I get to pick the place to eat."

That's Paul's meaning in verse 1. We could actually read "since" in the phrases: since you have encouragement from Christ to move you in this direction, since your hearts are secure and comforted in his love, since you sense the presence of the Spirit in your life and are aware of his promptings, since God has given you tender, compassionate hearts to move you toward kindness to each other, since God has made it possible for you to do it, "make my joy complete" by living in harmony with each other, "by being like-minded, having the same love, being one in spirit and of one mind." The crowning glory of a church is that its members live in loving harmony with each other.

But what exactly produces this harmony? What specifically brings it about? When there are disagreements, differences of opinion as to how things should be done, misunderstandings, and even personal slights, what enables a church to continue in love and unity?

The answer? There's harmony in the church when there's humility in the people. There's harmony in the church when each member determines to place the welfare of others ahead of his own, when each member willingly decides that the interests and needs of others will come ahead of his own.

That's what Paul goes on to say. After writing "Make my joy complete by living in harmony with each other," he goes on to specifically tell them how to make that happen—"Act with humility toward each other."

> *Do nothing out of selfish ambition or vain conceit. Rather, in humility value others above yourselves, not looking to your own interests but each of you to the interests of the others.* (2:3–4)

"Selfish ambition" is *what* I want, while "vain conceit" is the *reason* I want it. I want to be prominent (selfish ambition) because I'm more deserving (vain conceit). I want others to yield to what I say (selfish ambition) because my thoughts, my desires, and my happiness matter more than theirs (vain conceit). I want my way (selfish ambition) because of my importance (vain conceit). This is the spirit that causes dissension, creates conflict, and leads to splits or departures.

Humility is just the opposite. Humility leads to harmony. Humility says, "It doesn't have to be my way, because I can see that others would benefit from your way." Humility says, "Things don't necessarily have to please me, because I can see that they're meeting the needs of others." Humility says, "The music is not what I'd prefer, the board decision kind of goes against what I'd like, the refreshments are not handled the way I'd do it, but that's okay, because what *I* want is not the deciding factor; what's good for *others* is."

Humility thinks of others, and values others, ahead of oneself. Humility says, "Your needs and interests come ahead of mine. They matter more than mine do." Humility is not thinking less of yourself; it's simply thinking of yourself less.

Humility says, "My voice may be better, but you need to sing this solo in order to develop your gifts." Humility says, "I can probably lead the meeting better, but the people are more likely to accept the decision if they hear it coming from you." Humility says, "I think I just got the raw end of a deal, but that's okay, because what happens to me is not the main thing; keeping harmony in the church is more important."

When there's that kind of humility in the people—each one considering others more deserving than himself, each one looking more to the interests and needs of others—there's harmony in the church.

And that brings a lot of joy to every pastor!

7

DOWN THE LADDER TO THE HIGHEST PLACE

Philippians 2:5–11

(A six-foot stepladder is visible on the left side of the stage.)

After my first year of graduate studies in Texas, I drove back to California for the summer—a two-day drive providing you drive about fourteen hours per day. The mid-point stopping place for the night is Deming, New Mexico. I was single, I didn't have much money, and I didn't want to spend much on my motel that night. So I stayed in a "roach motel" in Deming, New Mexico. Literally, it was a roach motel—I had to put my shoes on the bed so that the roaches on the floor would not get into them that night.

At the end of that summer Nell and I married. On the return trip across the states back to Texas, we stopped again in Deming, New Mexico. For some reason, we didn't stay in that roach motel; we stayed in the next step up—Motel 6.

As the years have gone by, Nell and I have moved up. We went from Motel 6 to Best Western. And from Best Western, we're now at Embassy Suites. I suppose the next step up will be the Hilton or the Ritz Carlton.

There's always some ladder to climb *(pull the ladder to center stage)*, and the higher up the ladder we go, the more status we have.

We rent an apartment—one room—with a roommate to share costs. Several years later we buy an inexpensive condo. Then we get married and scrape enough together to buy a fixer-upper. Years later we trade up to a three-bedroom, two-bath, 1,800-square-foot home. And somewhere in the future is that prestigious zip code, with 3,500 square feet, or that luxury apartment within a block of the ocean.

We make the team, we get into two games as a sub, we're first string, we're all conference, we get a scholarship to college, All-American, first round draft pick, All-Pro, Hall of Fame. There's always some ladder to climb.

In a few weeks my school will have a graduation. All the spectators are seated on the lawn. The faculty and students are lining up for the march in. At the very back of the line is the new college graduate—flimsy black robe, not much thicker than a hospital gown, plain black hat, black tassel. In front of them are the junior faculty, those who don't yet have their doctorate degrees. In front of them are the regular faculty—thick robes with the three black-felt bars on the arms signifying doctorate degrees. See the color of their hoods reflecting their schools and their academic disciplines. See the fancy kind of hats they wear. In front of the regular faculty are the department chairs, those who will read the various graduating names (that's me!). But in front of me are the deans of the various schools, the ones who will sit on the platform: the dean of the School of Theology, the dean of the School of Business, the dean of the School of Education, the dean of the School of Psychology. And at the very front of the line, leading in the whole procession—the president, with his gold medallion; and the commencement speaker—somebody famous.

There's always some ladder to climb, and the higher up we go, the more status we have: general admission seats in the right field bleachers, season tickets behind third base, private luxury boxes with air conditioning and food service.

Kmart shoes, Penney's pumps, Nordstrom's Eccos, and then some designer names I can't even pronounce—Manileto?

The higher we go, the more status we have. And the status feels good. It makes us feel important. It gets us attention.

And if we don't have enough status, we'll even make some up. Three dogs meet. The first dog says to the other two, "My name is Fifi—that's

F-I-F-I." The second dog says, "My name is Mimi—that's M-I-M-I." The third dog says, "My name is Fido—that's P-H-A-E-D-E-A-U-X."

Two men meet. One says to the other, "What do you do for a living?" "I'm a sanitation engineer." "Oh, you're a janitor." "Yeah, well, what do you do for a living?" "I'm a ventilating specialist." "Oh, you're a window washer."

Two pastors meet. One says to the other, "How big is your church?" Hmm, what number should I give him? The number of people who were in the sanctuary last Sunday? That's not a very big number. Maybe I should include all the children who were in other rooms at the same time. Ah, that's still not very many. I know, I'll give him our mailing-list number—the people who've come to the church at one time or another. That's a big number, and he'll be impressed.

We want that status, and we want to climb the ladder to get to the highest spot—for self-importance, to be thought of as somebody, and to have others pay attention to us. It feels good to be looked up to, to be catered to, and to be thought of as special.

But that concern for status is troublesome and dangerous because it tends to put "me first." "I'm higher up, so do it my way. I matter more, so please me. I'm more important, so serve my interests."

And if that attitude creeps into the church—"Do it my way, please me, serve my interests"—the result is conflict, argument, dissension, and rupture.

To save his friends from that kind of conflict and separation, the apostle Paul writes to them, "Don't be concerned about how far up the ladder you can go. Instead, think of how far down you can come. Your aim is not to climb up but to climb down."

He writes this to his friends in the city of Philippi. "Each of you should care most of all about others, not about yourself." "Value others above yourselves, not looking to your own interests but each of you to the interests of others" (2:3a–4).

And then he gives them an example. "Your example," he says, "is Christ. He went down the ladder for the sake of others. He went to the lowest level because he cared about the interests of others."

As we live with each other in church, our model is not someone in our culture who ascended the ladder, not someone who went from the bottom to the top—the mailroom boy who became CEO, the sub who became MVP, the immigrant who struck it rich. As we live with each other and as we act toward each other, our model is one who descended the ladder, one who went from the top to the bottom—from omnipotence to obscurity, from stardom to slavery, from riches to rags. Our model is Christ, who came down the ladder for our sake, down to the lowest level because he cared about our interests. That's the attitude we should have toward each other. "In your relationships with one another, have the same mindset as Christ Jesus" (2:5).

Let's consider this mindset, this attitude, this model in its fullness. Let's see how far down the ladder Christ came for our sake—the level he stooped to—in order that we might forever rid ourselves of pride and selfish ambition and vain conceit. Let's follow Paul's description of how far Christ came in order to see how far we, too, should go.

Paul wrote that Christ started at the highest spot *(climb the ladder to the high rung)*—which was equality with God. He was equal with God: "Who, being in very nature God, did not consider equality with God something to be used to his own advantage" (2:6).

Christ sat on the throne of heaven with the Father. The angels adored him and bowed before him. In his very nature, he was the same as God. Deep inside, in the essence of his being, he was God. He was the one who spread out the brilliant galaxies for the Trinity's enjoyment. He was the one who created the earth and formed the people to live on it in order that he and the Father could love them with the same love they had for each other and in order that someday they could share heaven with him.

But when his people sinned and their sin stained them, when it was no longer possible to bring them to glory because their sin would be a pulsating evil and stench in heaven—he immediately knew that his equality with God was not "something to be used to his own advantage." It was not for his benefit; it was not something to be enjoyed for his own sake but something to be used for their interests.

The very nature of God is not to be a getter but a giver. To be equal with God means you're not one who grasps; you're one who goes. Because the only way to get rid of sin and its consequences was to go and live there among them and pay their penalty for them.

And only God could do that. Only God could live perfectly among them and not end up having his own sin to pay for. Only God could live free of the penalty of death and therefore take their penalty on himself.

The Son looked at the Father and did not consider his equality with God something to be held onto for his own interests but rather something to be used to serve others. And so he made himself nothing, and he stepped into their world to serve their interests *(climb down a rung):* "he made himself nothing by taking the very nature of a servant, being made in human likeness" (2:7).

He made himself nothing. He didn't come as a king into his own creation. He didn't birth himself into the ruling Roman empire of the world. He didn't choose a middle-class family with the financial means to give him a head start in society.

He made himself nothing. He put himself in the hands of a poor couple, in a conquered nation, in a backwater town that was the Tijuana of his day— Nazareth. The other cities around turned up their noses and said, "Can any good thing come out of Nazareth?"

He made himself nothing because deep in his being, he was taking on the essence of a servant. Just as at the core of his nature he was equal with God, so now at the core of his nature he was going to be a servant. And he would totally take on the likeness of humanity. He would get hungry and tired. He would hurt when the splinters went into his palm. He'd feel the pain when his friends betrayed him. When all of them thought it was above them to do a servant's job of washing dirty feet before a dinner, he'd get the towel, and he'd kneel on the floor. He'd understand their weaknesses and serve them anyway. He made himself nothing, because deep in his being, he was going to serve.

But how far would he go to serve their interests? How much would he do? How much of himself would he give? Would he think of himself just a little bit? Would he retain just a small amount of what he might be entitled to? Would he at least hold himself on a par with the others in his circle? Or would he humble himself even further? Would he lower himself even more for their sake? Would he die for them? Would he let himself be killed so that they could live? *(Another rung down, to the floor)* "And being found in appearance as a man, he humbled himself by becoming obedient to death—even death on a cross!" (2:8).

He would follow through on what he came for—he would voluntarily die for them. If his service were to matter, it would have to go that far because his death was the only thing that could remove their sin. He would have to take their sin on himself and let it crush him instead of them.

He would die in the most humiliating and painful way that has ever been conceived—on a cross. Humiliating, because it was used only for foreign terrorists, notorious criminals, and rebellious slaves. Painful, because large nails severed tendons and splintered bones, the body sagged, and hour after hour it became harder to breathe as you slowly suffocated to death.

He died because you are a sinner, and he loved you and did not want you to perish. He cared for you ahead of himself, and he died for you and me. Charles Wesley tried to capture it in a hymn we sing:

> He left his Father's throne above,
> > so free, so infinite his grace.
> Emptied himself of all but love,
> > and bled for Adam's helpless race.
> 'Tis mercy all, immense and free,
> > for O my God, it found out me.
> Amazing love, how can it be,
> > that Thou my God shouldst die for me.

That's what this table is about. He died for you. This is his body, which was broken for you. This is his blood, which was shed for you. It was for you. *(Lead the congregation in observing the Lord's Supper.)*

When his downward descent had reached the furthest depths it could go, when he died a criminal's death and was buried in a borrowed grave—a forgotten servant, abandoned, ignored by most—when he did all he came to do and it cost him his life to do it, when his caring for the interests of others had taken *his* life but had brought *them* to God, when it looked like the bottom would swallow him forever, God raised him up. God exalted him.

(Climb back up the ladder, one rung at a time, as each verse is read:)

> *Therefore God exalted him to the highest place*
> *and gave him the name that is above every name,*
> *that at the name of Jesus every knee should bow,*
> *in heaven and on earth and under the earth,*
> *and every tongue acknowledge that Jesus Christ is Lord,*
> *to the glory of God the Father.* (2:9–11)

He descended to the lowest level, and "God exalted him to the highest place." And then God gave him the name that is above every name, the name Yahweh. God gave him his own name, the most honored name in all of creation, the name by which he referred to himself, so that whenever someone says, "Jesus," all of creation will say, "Lord!* Jesus Christ is Lord. Jesus Christ is Yahweh God!"

And as he stands in his glory, every knee will bend in submission, every head will bow in acknowledgement of his name—all the angels in heaven, all the races on earth, all the seething demons under the earth. Every knee down, every tongue acknowledging that Jesus Christ is Lord, to the glory of God the Father.

If we will share his humility, we will share his glory. If we go down the ladder, God will raise us up. *(Climb down, one rung for each verse in verses 3–5:)*

> *Do nothing out of selfish ambition or vain conceit. Rather, in humility value others above yourselves, not looking to your own interests but each of you to the interests of others. In your relationships with one another, have the same mindset as Christ Jesus.* (2:3–5)

Prayer: Lord, in our churches, keep our hearts caring more for each other than for ourselves. In the name of him who *died* for us, Amen.

---

* In the Old Testament, Yahweh usually appears as "Lord." In the New Testament, it appears simply as "Lord."

8

WORKING OUT THE WORKING IN

Philippians 2:12–18

Let's suppose I'm getting together for lunch with Daniel, the worship leader, to talk over some special services that are coming up at the church. We agree to meet at a coffee shop.

We walk in, and I get ready to signal "two" to the hostess, but she's not looking at me. She's looking down because the manager is scolding her. And we hear him: "How many times have I told you not to seat people until the table is cleared? Wait until it's bussed and wiped. That's not too hard to remember, is it? Don't let it happen again."

He walks away, and I signal her "two." She grabs a couple of menus and says, "Follow me." As we walk toward a table, she says, "He's such an idiot. He got promoted to manager last month, and he thinks he's such a big shot. Well, he's not; he's turning everybody off. Two waitresses have quit, and I know two more who are thinking of it, and I'm talking to a temp agency. Here's your table. Notice it's cleared off!" The hostess leaves.

Soon our waitress comes by. "Hasn't your busboy brought water yet? Tsk! I don't know why I have to do his work and mine too. Alex, can you get some waters and table settings here? I'll give you a couple of minutes to look over the menu, and then I'll come back for your order."

The busboy, Alex, comes by with the waters and the table settings— napkins, knife, fork, spoon. As he's laying them out, he says, "She's supposed to share her tips with me, but I think she's stiffing me. When I bus her tables, I see what people ordered. I know what kind of tips there should be. She's supposed to give me a percent of that, but I don't think she is. I've half a mind to let her set her own tables." He leaves.

In a minute the waitress comes back. "What'll ya have?" I order a Cobb salad. Daniel asks about the pot roast—"Is it good?" "Ehhh, it's okay." Daniel chooses the BLT instead. "Whadda you want to drink?" she says. Daniel orders a Diet Coke; I ask for coffee. Pretty soon she's back with his Diet Coke but no coffee—"They forgot to start a new pot. I have to do everything around here. It'll be a couple of minutes on your coffee."

Our table is not very far from the area where the chefs are, inside under the lamps, doing the cooking. When the plates are ready, they put them on the shelf for the waitresses to take to the tables. We overhear two waitresses arguing at the shelf: "That was my hamburger order you took. Wait for your own order to come up. Next time you take my order, I'm going to sneak some Tabasco into your spaghetti sauce, and then let's see what kind of a tip you get!"

Just then another waitress comes up to the shelf and complains to the chef. "What's taking so long on my meatloaf? Let's get some efficiency in there. Man, what do they teach you in cooking school?"

Daniel and I finish our lunch, and we leave. We've talked through some of our business, but each of us has to contact some other people or look into some details. So we need to meet again in a week to finish up. Out in the parking lot, before we get in our cars, we decide to pick the time and place for next week. "Where shall we have lunch? Shall we come back here?"

"Noooo." No, we don't want to come back here. They're fighting, complaining, bickering, and squabbling. They don't like each other, and they don't like working there. When you're complaining and arguing, you drive the crowd away.

We see another coffee shop about a block down the street. "How about we meet there next week?" "Yeah, okay, let's meet there. Not here."

Next week we walk into the second coffee shop. The manager is standing by the hostess, talking to her. But he stops to greet us. "Welcome, gentlemen. Two for lunch? LuAnn will seat you right away." And then he finishes his conversation with the hostess. "LuAnn, you're doing a great job. You have a good way with the customers. Keep checking to see that the tables are cleared before you seat them. The family that just left—they told me what a great help you were in getting the booster chair for their child. Good work."

She takes us to our booth, and as we slide in, she says, "Enjoy your lunch, gentlemen."

Our waitress comes by and notices that we don't have any water or table settings. "Oh my, let me get those for you. The busboy for this section is doing double duty today. One of our other busboys called in sick, and Carlos is trying to cover two sections. We're all glad he's such a hard worker. Carlos, I got these. You go ahead and clear Judy's table."

"Can I get you gentlemen anything to drink?" Daniel orders his Diet Coke, and I order my coffee. In a minute she's back with his Diet Coke but no coffee. "Our coffee's so popular, it goes fast. The pot was down to about one-half inch. I could have brought that to you, but I wanted to make you a fresh pot. It'll be just a minute."

We order. I order the Cobb salad again. Daniel asks about the chicken potpie. "One of my favorites," the waitress says. "Flaky crust, big hunks of chicken. You'll love it."

For dessert, I notice they have a new item—bread pudding squares, drizzled with caramel, with a cup of some kind of cinnamon-apple syrup-sauce to dip into along with a big scoop of ice cream and two large dollops of whipped cream. Man, that looks good. I decide I've had too many rabbit-food salads. "Hey, Daniel, ya wanna share one of these?" "Yeah, Don, let's get one."

The waitress comes by. "Ma'am, we'd like to share one of these desserts."

"Oh, I don't blame you. I'm always tempted when I bring one of those. If you notice that one of the bread pudding squares is missing when I bring the plate, that's because I usually taste one in advance to make sure it's just right for my customers."

After we're done, out in the parking lot, Daniel and I look at each other. "Hey, this is a nice place. Let's keep in it mind for next time."

"You bet."

When you're complaining and arguing, you drive the crowd away. When you're grateful and gracious, you draw them in.

Let's suppose a visitor comes to your church. They've gotten a flyer in the mail about a special series of messages that are starting, and they decide to visit. Since it's their first time, they're a little late. So they slip in the back and get a seat on the side. Hearing about the refreshments afterwards, they make their way to the fellowship area.

As they look over the table with everything on it, one of the ladies standing near them says, "Isn't this wonderful? Look at all of these goodies. Most of them are homemade. Every week it's different. You never know what it'll be. Help yourself. Oh, especially try some of those—I know who made them; you'll love them."

The visitor fills his plate and wanders away from the table. A couple of men come up to talk to him. The visitor is still impressed with the food: "Who arranges this?"

"Oh, the women plan it. I think maybe it rotates by months. I'm not sure. Different people bring things. People here are great; good things just sort of seem to happen."

Someone else comes up to him. "Did you see that there's coffee over there in the corner?"

"No, I didn't. That sounds good."

"Let me help you get some." And they walk toward the coffee.

As the coffee is pouring into the cup and cream and sugar are being stirred in, the visitor mentions that a friend of his visited the previous week and said that the church had terrific musicians on the platform. His friend particularly mentioned a young piano player who did something marvelous on the piano during the offering. But today's piano player didn't look very young.

"No, he has grown kids. But he's our regular piano player. The one your friend mentioned last week was filling in because our regular one was recovering from some surgery. Can you imagine a church like ours having two such great piano players? We have the best music. Did you like the drums and guitars, and the way the singers blended their voices?"

The visitor takes his coffee and goes to sit by himself against one of the walls. He looks at what he sees—people sitting and talking, people hugging, people holding each other's children, people quietly cleaning up a spill and straightening the tables. The visitor thinks to himself, "There's something about them. They enjoy each other."

In a few moments someone else comes to sit by him. And the visitor asks, "How long has your pastor been here?"

The member says, "About seven to eight months. Oh, let me tell you about our pastor. *(Exaggerating)*. He is soooo wonderful. He's absolutely the very best speaker you've ever heard. And did you notice how handsome he is? And he's kind to animals and little children. And he . . ."

When you're complaining and arguing, you drive the people away. When you're grateful and gracious, you draw them in. When a visitor sees the members loving each other and caring about each other, the visitor says, "God is in this place."

That's the encouragement Paul gives to his friends in a small church in the city of Philippi. "Be grateful and gracious to each other," he writes. "Let there be no complaining or squabbling among you. You're God's family; you're his children. You're brothers and sisters with the same Father. Let others see what the family of God is like so that they'll want to be part of it. Be grateful and gracious to each other so that you can shine forth the Word of Life that will save others."

When we're grateful and gracious to one another, two things happen. First, unbelievers are drawn to the gospel. They see something different, and they're drawn to God's life. When a church is grateful and gracious, it glows for the gospel:

> *Do everything without grumbling or arguing, so that you may become blameless and pure, "children of God without fault in a warped and crooked generation." Then you will shine among them like stars in the sky as you hold firmly to the word of life.* (2:14–16a)

When we're grateful and gracious, Paul says, not complaining or squabbling, we "shine" like bright stars in a dark night as we testify to the gospel. Visitors or unbelievers see how we treat each other, and they're drawn to us because they never see that kind of love and kindness and gentleness anywhere else. Everything else around them is crooked and perverse, harsh, and hurtful.

They don't see that kind of love and kindness in their families—they see spite and arguing, anger and hate, shouting and cruel comments. But they see that this family is different.

They don't see that kind of gentleness and graciousness at their work—they see cutthroat tactics and cattiness, underhandedness and deceit, crudeness and harassment. This place is different.

They see something they don't see anywhere else, and they're drawn to God's life.

When we're grateful and gracious, we glow for the gospel. We shine the light of God into a dark world, and we draw people into God's family.

There's a second thing that happens when we're grateful and gracious to one another—joy permeates the church; there's gladness all around. The absence of complaining and squabbling, the awareness that we are God's children, and the evidence of God's life—these things bring joy to everyone, to the leaders and to the whole congregation.

That's what Paul goes on to say. "If you live with gratitude and grace toward each other, I'll be full of joy because I'll know that I didn't labor in vain and that my ministry was worth it all. And even if my imprisonment results in death, I'll feel like I've had a small part in what you've become before God. And I'll be thrilled, and you also will join in my joy." Joy all around:

> I will be able to boast on the day of Christ that I did not run or labor in vain. But even if I am being poured out like a drink offering on the sacrifice and service coming from your faith, I am glad and rejoice with all of you. So you too should be glad and rejoice with me. (2:16b–18)

It's possible Paul may die soon. That's what he means in verse 17 when he says, "even if I am being poured out like a drink offering on the sacrifice and service coming from your faith." His imagery comes from when a sacrifice was offered to God. It was put on the altar, and the fire beneath it created an aroma that rose toward the heavens. It was customary to pour some wine or oil on the sacrifice—to add a liquid offering, a drink offering—to complete the fragrance or aroma. "Maybe that's what's going to happen in the next few months," he says. "Maybe my imprisonment will result in my death. But if that's the case, it'll simply be my last small part added to what you have become before God. And I'll be so pleased."

A church that lives in harmony and humility brings joy to the leaders and to everyone in the congregation. A grateful and gracious church glows for the gospel and guarantees gladness.

That's what we want in our churches today. And the good thing is, that's what God will help us have. God himself is working that in us in order that we can work it out among us. He's put within us the desire and ability to live in harmony and humility. And we work out what God is working in.

That's how Paul began this section of his letter. He started off by saying, "Translate into reality what God is already doing in your heart. Work out what God is working in":

> *Therefore, my dear friends, as you have always obeyed—not only in my presence, but now much more in my absence—continue to work out your salvation with fear and trembling, for it is God who works in you to will and to act in order to fulfill his good purpose.* (2:12–13)

"I'm not there with you, so let me hear that this is happening among you. Work out what God is working in."

Notice his words carefully in verse 12. He doesn't say, "Work *for* your salvation." He doesn't say, "Work *on* your salvation." No, he says, "Work *out* the salvation that is in you."

You don't work *for* your salvation. You don't do something to please God so that he will save you. Your salvation is a gift that comes to you freely when you trust in Jesus' death to pay the penalty for your sins. No work of your own could ever balance out your penalty. The only way you could ever be saved is for Jesus to step in with his sinless life and pay your penalty for you. And if you trust him for that, God gives you salvation—a free gift that you didn't work for or earn.

But once you have your salvation, you live it out. You work *out* the salvation that is inside you. And everything that God wants you to do, he's helping you to do it. You find you have a desire inside to do it; God gave you that desire. And you sense you have the ability to do it; God put that ability there. That's what Paul means when he says in verse 13, "it is God who works in you to will and to act according to his good purpose." God works in us to desire and to carry out the good purpose he has for us—to live in harmony and humility with each other. And as we keep on working *out* what he's working *in*, and as we do all things without complaining and squabbling, we'll shine like stars in a dark world, showing his life to others and bringing joy to ourselves.

9

"WE DON'T HAVE MEN LIKE THAT"

Philippians 2:19–30

(The pastor enters as Octavian, a Praetorian Guard, coming into the squad room after a six-hour guard duty chained to Paul in Paul's rented house. One end of the chain is still attached to his right wrist. Another soldier, Marcus [imagined], is on a bench sharpening his sword.)

Hey, Marcus, how ya doing? Hey, your sword is sharp enough. You ought to be oiling your shield instead.

No, I don't have any more oil. I think Sergius does, though, in his locker. I don't think he'll mind if you borrow some.

Hey, help me get this chain off first, will ya? . . . Thanks.

Yeah, I've been with that Paul guy again—chained to him six hours every other day for the past three weeks. I don't know how to figure him out. He doesn't act like a man who's going to be on trial for his life in the next couple of months. He gets a lot of visitors to that house he's renting. But when they talk about the trial, I get the impression it doesn't really matter to Paul how it comes out. He keeps talking about a win–win situation—he wins if he's set free, and he wins if he's executed. One way he goes back to what he was doing; the other way he goes up to be with this King he's always talking about.

I said to him once, "You don't look too worried for a man who could die in the next few months."

He said, "Octavian, you have no idea how excited I am about what's happening right now. You know why I'm in these chains, don't you?"

"Yeah, you're charged with claiming allegiance to some King other than Caesar. If that's true, Paul, your chances at trial are pretty slim."

"Well," he said, "in a way, the charge is true, and in a way, it isn't. Right now he's a heavenly King. And one day he'll rule the world. But he's more than a King, Octavian. He's a Savior."

And then he started telling me how this King died on a cross with me in mind. And I said, "Whadda ya mean 'with me in mind.' I don't even know him." And he says, "But, Octavian, he knows you. He knows all the wrong you've done. He knows how it eats you up inside and how you fear the day you're going to have to pay for all of it. And, Octavian, he died to pay that penalty for you. If you believe in him, Octavian, he'll save you from the consequences of your sin." And he told me to talk to you, Marcus.

You're kidding! You've bought into it? He said there's a whole bunch of us guards who've believed. So you're one of them! Well, it must have done you some good. From what I hear from some of the other guys, you used to be a real hell-raiser. And rumor is that in combat, you didn't distinguish too carefully between civilians and soldiers. Tough luck for whoever got in the way of your sword. Yeah, you're different now.

Anyway, Paul said he was excited about what was going on, not just because of the effect on some of us guards but also because apparently there are a lot of other people here in Rome who feel as he does, and they're starting to speak up more. Evidently the message of this King of his is getting out.

Did he tell you about the letter he's writing? . . . Oh, I guess he must have just started it yesterday. When I went on duty today, he was in the middle of it. I asked him, "Who are you writing to?" He said, "To some friends in the city of Philippi. They sent money so that I could keep renting this house, and I wanted to thank them. I also hear they're having a tough time—some people in their city are making life difficult for them—and I just wanted to tell them to hang in there. Octavian, do you mind putting the chain on my left arm so that I can write with my right?" That's why it was on my right wrist when I came here to the squad room.

Anyway, he spent most of the day writing, so we didn't talk much. There were a couple of other guys in the room the whole time. I've seen them there with him a lot. Do you know who I mean? One of them is I'd say mid-to-late twenties, name . . . Timothy. The other one is older, name . . . Epifrodo? . . . Epaphroditus?! Man, I got that one wrong. Anyway, these two guys were there with him. They've been there every time I've gone for the past couple of weeks.

You know, you'd think you could learn a lot about people if you're watching them six hours a day, three to four times a week for several weeks. But I can't figure those two guys out either.

Take the younger one, Timothy. He and Paul seem to know each other really well. From what I gather, the two of them have done a lot of traveling together over the past several years. At first I thought he was Paul's son, the way he seemed to take care of whatever Paul needed and serve as his contact or go-between with people outside the house. I asked Paul, "Is he your son?" He said, "No, not physically, but for all practical purposes, I consider him my son. I can see why you might think he is because of the way he acts toward me, like a son to his father.

"Octavian, I don't know another young man like him. He cares about this King I've been telling you about as much as I do. And all he wants to do is make him known to others. I first met him several years ago on my third trip to his hometown, Lystra. I'd been in Lystra a couple of times earlier, and by the time I came for my third visit, there was a pretty good-sized church there. He was one of the young men in the church. His mother and grandmother were believers and active in the church, but his dad didn't have too much to do with it. Anyway, Timothy was in his early twenties then, and everyone in the church spoke well of him. They told me he had been waiting for me to come because he wanted to join me in my travels to other towns to get out the message.

"At first I was hesitant. I didn't know him. It seemed unusual for a young man to want to do that. A lot of young men are just kind of into the toga scene, if you know what I mean. They just want to have fun. A few of them are starting to think about their careers. But mostly they're fairly self-centered, kind of focused on themselves. But Timothy seemed different.

He seemed to care more about the needs and interests of others. So I took him with me. . . .

"These people I'm writing to in Philippi—he was with me the first time I came to their city. And once I see how my trial's going, I'm going to send him back to them with the news. Look what I wrote here. I'm telling them to expect him." He showed it to me:

> I hope in the Lord Jesus to send Timothy to you soon, that I also may be cheered when I receive news about you. I have no one else like him, who will show genuine concern for your welfare. For everyone looks out for their own interests, not those of Jesus Christ. But you know that Timothy has proved himself, because as a son with his father he has served with me in the work of the gospel. I hope, therefore, to send him as soon as I see how things go with me. And I am confident in the Lord that I myself will come soon. (2:19–24)

Paul said, "As soon as I see how things go, Octavian, I'm going to send Timothy to Philippi. If the verdict goes against me, he'll tell them that, and he'll keep them strong. If I'm acquitted, he'll take them the good news and let them know I'm on my way to see them as soon as possible. One way or another, he's the person to send to Philippi. He cares about them as much as I do. He's proved himself to them. They'll listen to him, and he'll convey what I want to them. Octavian, do you know how rare it is to find a man who genuinely cares more about others than himself? Who's more committed to their needs and interests than he is to his own? Do you know how rare it is to find a man like that?"

I didn't answer him, Marcus, because I don't get it. Man, I'm in this army for what I can get out of it. I'm looking for fast promotions, and I'll do whatever it takes to get them—a little flattery to the commander, some holiday gifts to his wife, volunteering for double shifts. Man, I want up the ladder, and you gotta make that happen for yourself!

I don't understand this Timothy. Assuming this King and gospel business of theirs is going to grow and maybe amount to something, Timothy ought to stay here in Rome and not let Paul send him to some backwater Philippi. I mean, Rome is where it's at. If Timothy has any ambition, if he wants to be a leader in the movement, this is the place to be. What does Paul call their groups when they get together—churches? Well, Rome is where the big churches are going to be. From what I gather, Timothy could be one of the up-and-comers here in Rome. Getting sent to a little group eight hundred miles away from the action is not how to make it happen. Talk about a bad career move!

I told Paul that, "Paul, you're sending him into limbo. You ought to help him climb the ladder. Instead, you're pointing him down. That doesn't make sense!"

And he said, "Octavian, our King came down the ladder to serve us. Up in heaven he was equal with God, but he made himself nothing for our sakes because he cared more about us than himself. And now our only ambition is to serve him and others. These people in Philippi need to do that; some of them need to care more about others than they do about themselves. And when Timothy comes to them, they'll see another example of what that looks like. When he arrives, they can't help but realize he's more interested in their welfare than his own ambition and advancement. Ambition, Octavian? Our only ambition is to serve our King."

He could see I wasn't getting it. So he pointed to the other fellow in the room—Epifro—? Epaphroditus. Man, I'll never get it.

Anyway, he said, "Octavian, do you see the other fellow sitting over there?" "Yeah." "He's the one who brought me the money from Philippi. When I finish this letter, I'm going to give it to him to take back home. His friends back in Philippi are worried about him; they hear he's been ill. He hasn't seen what I've written yet—look, I just finished this paragraph."

But I think it is necessary to send back to you Epaphroditus, my brother, coworker and fellow soldier, who is also your messenger, whom you sent to take care of my needs. For he longs for all of you and is distressed because you heard he was ill. Indeed he was ill, and almost died. But God had mercy on him, and not on him only but also on me, to spare me sorrow upon sorrow. Therefore I am all the more eager to send him, so that when you see him again you may be glad and I may have less anxiety. So then, welcome him in the Lord with great joy, and honor people like him, because he almost died for the work of Christ. He risked his life to make up for the help you yourselves could not give me. (2:25–30)

And then Paul continued, "Did you know that, Octavian—that he almost died bringing the money to me? He started out with it from Philippi; it takes about six weeks to cover the eight hundred miles to Rome—sailing from Macedonia, around Greece, and on to Rome, with lots of port stops along the way. Well, about one week into the trip, he started running a high fever. He should have immediately turned back. But he didn't. He knew I needed the money. It's a large sum—it'll pay the rent on this house for two years—so he was determined to get it to me. Well, another week on ship, and now the fever was causing severe headaches, and he was vomiting, dry heaves. He should have gotten off that ship and onto land, where he could get some medical attention. But he kept coming—he knew my lease payment was coming up, and if the money didn't get here, I'd be thrown in a dungeon where I could die even before my trial. Another week on ship, then he was coughing up blood, he couldn't keep anything down, and he'd lost thirty pounds. Octavian, he almost died. He risked his life for the work of his King. Would you risk your life for your king?"

I didn't answer him, Marcus. Would I risk my life for Caesar? I'm a soldier. I'm part of his personal bodyguard. Would I take a spear for Caesar? If it came down to it, I don't know. That's what I'm paid to do. But if I wasn't paid to do it, is Caesar worth my life?

Marcus, I'm at the other end of all of this. Instead of dying for my king, I think if I was Epaphroditus, and I was on a ship with that much money— two years' worth of rent—I think I'd jump ship the first chance I had and retire to the Riviera. I'd live it up away from my king, Marcus. I'd never give my life for him if I didn't have to.

I don't get these guys, Marcus. Timothy has no ambition but to serve their King. Epaphrotidus is ready to die for their King. And Paul can think of nothing happier than to be with their King. I don't get it, Marcus. We don't have men like that.

What? . . . Yeah, you're right. . . . We don't have a King like that.

10

THE CHRISTIAN SUBCULTURE: RIGHTEOUS OR RUBBISH?

Philippians 3:1–9

Sometimes in our good churches—our solid, evangelical, biblically-committed churches—we feel pressured to act in certain ways, to fit in with certain norms, and to participate in certain activities. It's a subtle pressure, but it carries with it the idea that if you really want to be pleasing to God, these are the things you'll do, these are the ways you'll act, and these are the activities you'll engage in.

For example, you'll be expected to belong to a particular political party and participate in certain social protests. You'll have acceptable opinions about such things as capital punishment, gun control, welfare, immigration, environmental issues, the legalization of marijuana, America's overseas conflicts, homeschooling, rock concerts, which parts of your body it's okay to poke holes in, which beverages you can drink, and whether it's appropriate to go to Las Vegas.

You'll be urged to tithe, to give ten percent of your income, to your local church. You can give extra sums to other missions or charitable organizations, but the tithe itself needs to go to your home church.

You'll have a time of devotions and prayer every day, for at least fifteen to twenty minutes, preferably in the morning, as a necessary condition for really walking with God.

You'll regularly and actively witness to your neighbors or somebody at work, engaging them in conversations and inviting them to church.

It's kind of a Christian subculture, an evangelical lifestyle, a set of be-havioral expectations, that we feel is being imposed on us. And the implica-tion is that if you follow these rules and regulations, you can be confident that your Christian life is what God wants it to be. You'll know that you're pleasing him and are righteous in his eyes.

If you disagree about any of these things, and if you publicly voice your disagreement, others will probably think less of you. They'll question your spirituality and maybe even distance themselves a bit from you. It could result in arguments and dissension and eventually lead to factions and di-vision in the church.

In our good churches, there's often this Christian subculture, this sup-posed evangelical lifestyle. If you're the right kind of Christian, if you really want to please God, you'll do these things and think these things. And if you don't, others may pull away and distance themselves from you.

Years ago the apostle Paul discovered that the same thing was happen-ing in a church he loved more than any other. His dear friends in the church at Philippi were being pressured by a particular subculture. They, too, were being pressured to adopt a certain lifestyle with its particular rules and regulations.

Visiting missionaries and teachers from the mother-church in Je-rusalem had come to the city of Philippi. These teachers were Jewish be-lievers, Jewish Christians. And when they came to the Gentile Christians in Philippi, they started teaching these Gentile believers, "To be the best Christian possible, you need to live a Jewish lifestyle. To be absolutely con-fident that you're pleasing God, you need to follow the Jewish traditions that have come down through the centuries. In particular, you need to be circumcised, you need to keep the Old Testament laws, and you need to observe the ceremonial rituals—the holidays, the fasts, the washings."

These Jewish Christians were saying to the Gentile Christians, "It's won-derful that you Gentiles have believed in Jesus Christ and are saved. But if you want to fully please God, you also have to follow the ancient guidelines that God gave his people—the rules and regulations of the Old Testament. You need to keep the dietary kosher food laws, you need to observe the spe-cial days of the religious calendar, and most of all, you need to have all of your males circumcised as a sign that they are really committed. We Christians in the mother-church at Jerusalem are following these things. These are the specified behaviors that God wants all believers to follow. If you want to be confident of your spiritual life, if you want to fully please God and be righteous in his eyes, then these are the things you'll do."

In other words, they were trying to impose their Jewish lifestyle on the Gentile believers at Philippi. When the apostle Paul got wind of it, he was eight hundred hundred miles away, under house arrest in Rome, expecting to stand trial before Caesar in a few months. But some visitors from the church filled him in on what was happening. And when he heard about the pressure being put on his friends in Philippi, he immediately saw the dangers that would come, and he addressed the issue in a letter he was writing to them.

He had already urged them to be like-minded and to live in harmony and unity of spirit. His visitors had reported that there was an undercurrent of sniping, some polarizing, some internal factions and disunity. It was already apparent that the conflict over lifestyles was causing dissension and discord in the church. He had already urged them to do everything without grumbling or arguing as he attempted to pull them back from the danger of dissension and disunity that comes from imposing our spiritual lifestyle on others.

But there was also another danger that he saw, a damage even greater than dissension and discord in the church—and that was spiritual damage that would occur to each of them individually. In the strongest language possible, he warns them about it. "Don't let them define your spiritual behavior," he will write. "Don't let them tell you what you must do to be righteous in God's eyes. Don't let them impose their lifestyle or subculture on you. You'll suffer great damage if you do. You'll be greatly harmed. An overwhelming tragedy will occur in your Christian life."

What is this tragedy that occurs if we let someone impose their rules and regulations on us, pressuring us into their spiritual lifestyle? What is the harm, the damage we suffer when we begin to think that following someone else's codes will make us more righteous in God's eyes?

As Paul moves to the second half of his letter, he begins with a warning about the visiting teachers. He says to his friends, "I've written you before about this, but for your sakes, I'm going to write about it again. Don't let them pressure you into their lifestyle; don't let them impose their rules and regulations on your Christian life." And then he gives his own experience, his own history. "I've been there," he says. "I've lived that way. It doesn't work. It won't make you more spiritual. In fact, just the opposite—it'll harm you." And this brings him finally to the great damage, the overwhelming sorrow that comes into our life if we let others define what behavior will make us pleasing to God. And he tells us what that sorrow and damage is.

He begins with his warning. "Watch out for these Jewish Christians. I've written about this before. What they're telling you will not help you. Instead, it will harm you":

> *Further, my brothers and sisters, rejoice in the Lord! It is no trouble for me to write the same things to you again, and it is a safeguard for you. Watch out for those dogs, those evildoers, those mutilators of the flesh. For it is we who are the circumcision, we who serve God by his Spirit, who boast in Christ Jesus, and who put no confidence in the flesh.* (3:1–3)

He describes these visiting teachers in three ways—*dogs, evildoers,* and *mutilators of the flesh.*

Those *dogs.* He uses their own word against them. The Jews had always referred to the Gentiles as dogs—and by that they did not have in mind the pets that we have that we play with, keep in the house, and take on walks, but the dogs of their day—wild, vicious, snarling beasts that roamed the streets in packs, rooting around in the garbage, even ready to attack small children that strayed off by themselves. If you picture an out-of-control rabid Rottweiler, pit bull, or Doberman, you'll have an idea of how the Jews felt about the Gentiles—dangerous, undisciplined, and outside God's favor.

The Jewish teachers were saying to the Gentile Philippians, "Now that you're saved, you don't have to be that way any more—like a dangerous dog. You can adopt our righteous Jewish traditions."

Paul flips the label back onto these Jewish teachers. "It's these teachers who are the dogs. They're the ones who are dangerous. They're the ones who will tear you apart with their teaching. They're the ones you need to watch out for."

Secondly, he calls them *evildoers*. "The work they're doing is evil. It will injure you; it will harm you."

And third, he calls them *mutilators of the flesh*. "They're trying to get you circumcised. They think that circumcision will bring you some spiritual benefit. All it will do is mutilate your flesh. They tell you it's committing yourself to God and gaining his blessing. I tell you it's nothing more than cutting yourself and getting bloody.

"Watch out for these men. Don't let them talk you into these behaviors. You don't need these things to have confidence before God, to know that he's pleased with you. You already have his full approval. All that circumcision stood for you already have. All that circumcision symbolized—becoming part of God's people, committing your life to him, enjoying his blessings—is already true of you":

> For it is we who are the circumcision, we who serve God by his Spirit, who boast in Christ Jesus, and who put no confidence in the flesh. (3:3)

What defines you as belonging to God is not some external behavior. What defines you is the internal presence of the Spirit of God. He's totally changed everything about you and has become part of your life. And now you are pleasing to God, not because you follow certain rules and regulations but because your heart is committed to him.

You're pleasing to him not because you belong to a particular political party, but because you act justly and fairly and mercifully toward all those around you.

Perhaps your way of pleasing him is not through loud social protests, but instead by working quietly through legislation to bring his truth to our society.

You're not bound by anybody's rules as to how much you should give or who you should give it to. Instead, you let the Spirit of God prompt you to be generous in many directions.

Having a time of Bible study and prayer every day can be good, and some people will be led to do that. But the real issue is, do you love his Word, and do you long to spend time with him? If you do, then maybe an hour or two one day a week is as pleasing to God as fifteen minutes a day every day of the week.

There's not anything wrong with circumcising for religious reasons as long as it's something you choose to do rather than having it forced on you. Paul once arranged the circumcision of one of his Gentile friends so that they could minister freely among the Jews without offense (Acts 16:3). But we already have the identifying characteristic God looks for—we have the Spirit of God in our heart. And any behavior that the Spirit leads us to offer God is good. There's no set of rules and regulations that we *have* to observe to have confidence before God. There are no required behaviors that are necessary to be approved by him.

We have the Spirit of God to lead us. And along with him, only one focus is necessary, and that's Christ. He's all we need to be pleasing to God and righteous in his eyes. We boast in Christ. We rejoice in him. We define ourselves in him. Our identity is through him. Our status is because of him. He's all we need.

"We put no confidence in the flesh"—in these external activities or these imposed, man-made requirements. No other behavior adds anything. Nothing else is needed for God's approval.

That's Paul's warning. "Don't let these teachers tell you that you have to adopt their lifestyle to be spiritual. Don't let them tell you that there are particular behaviors that will make you pleasing to God. Don't let them tell you that you have to belong to their subculture to be fully righteous in his eyes."

And then he moves to his own experience, to his own history. "I've been there," he says. "I've lived in their subculture. I've spent a long time depending on those behaviors to make me pleasing to God. If they want to talk externals, if they want to talk rules and regulations, if they want to talk about having confidence because of the Jewish lifestyle, nobody did it better than I. I scored off the charts. I've got them all beat hands down." And he gives them his own history of depending on externals to earn points with God:

> *For it is we who are the circumcision, we who serve God by his Spirit, who boast in Christ Jesus, and who put no confidence in the flesh—though I myself have reasons for such confidence.*
>
> *If someone else thinks they have reasons to put confidence in the flesh, I have more: circumcised on the eighth day, of the people of Israel, of the tribe of Benjamin, a Hebrew of Hebrews; in regard to the law, a Pharisee; as for zeal, persecuting the church; as for righteousness based on the law, faultless.* (3:3–6)

"They think Jewishness is what counts. Man, I had it. 'Circumcised the eighth day.' I was born into it. I didn't get circumcised as an adult convert, which is what they're trying to talk you into. I was circumcised at birth.

"'Of the people of Israel, of the tribe of Benjamin.' They want to adopt you in as converted Gentiles; I was part of it by natural heredity. They want you to earn it; I inherited it. I can trace my ancestry to one of the most respected of all tribes—Benjamin."

Benjamin was special. He was the only one of Jacob's twelve children to be born in the Promised Land. Benjamin's warriors were famous for their bravery and military skill.

The nation's first king came from Benjamin. Jerusalem, the holy city, was located in Benjamin's territory. When the country split into the northern and southern kingdoms, only Benjamin stayed loyal with David's tribe of Judah. Paul was from Benjamin.

"I was 'a Hebrew of the Hebrews.' I spoke the language, I kept the customs, and I didn't let the secular culture corrupt me.

"I was born into it—'circumcised on the eighth day, of the people of Israel, of the tribe of Benjamin, a Hebrew of Hebrews.' And then I added to it. To this inheritance, I brought my own accomplishments, my own activities. I brought a set of behaviors that no one could match.

"You want to talk about living by the rules and regulations! I was a Pharisee. We Pharisees studied the Old Testament as carefully as anyone could. We knew everything it said, and we did everything it required.

"And then among the Pharisees, nobody was more committed, nobody had more *zeal* than I to protect our Jewish heritage. Nobody was more passionate or active to preserve it than I. In my early days, when I thought

Christianity was a threat to our ancient faith, I was no ivory tower academic. I got in the trenches and did everything I could to rid the world of those whom I thought at the time were heretics. I *persecuted* them and even went to other cities to arrest them and bring them back for trial.

"And when all was said and done—if anyone asked, 'Did Paul live up to our code of behavior? Did Paul follow our rules and regulations? Can Paul have confidence that he is righteous in God's eyes'—when all was said and done, 'as for righteousness based on the law, faultless.' If you can have it through rules and regulations, if you can have it through external behavior, then I did. I was blameless. I did it all."

That's Paul's past experience. He's been there. He's lived that way. For a long time he let his behavior be defined and evaluated by some external lifestyle.

But now as he looks back at that way of living, as he looks back at trying to earn points with God by living under an imposed set of rules, he says, "You may think you're gaining, but you're losing. You may think it's a profit, but it's a loss. You may think you're getting ahead, but you're really going in the hole. Instead of these behaviors making you righteous, they fill you with rubbish. There's no gain, only garbage."

And this brings him finally to the great damage, the great harm, the overwhelming tragedy that comes if you let someone else define what you need to do in order to please God and be righteous in his eyes.

If you let others impose their rules and regulations on you, you miss out on what life with Christ can really be like. If you let someone convince you that their spiritual set of behaviors is necessary, you miss out on how Christ wants to specifically develop your spiritual life. You end up with a righteousness that comes from keeping the rules, but you miss out on the real righteousness and acceptance that comes from walking in faith with Christ.

Living by all those behavioral standards turned out not to be a profit but a loss. Why? Because it took Paul's eyes off of the real life that Christ wanted to give him:

> But whatever were gains to me I now consider loss for the sake of Christ. What is more, I consider everything a loss because of the surpassing greatness of knowing Christ Jesus my Lord, for whose sake I have lost

all things. I consider them garbage, that I may gain Christ and be found in him, not having a righteousness of my own that comes from the law, but that which is through faith in Christ—the righteousness that comes from God on the basis of faith. (3:7–9)

When you live by other people's standards, you start out thinking, "This will profit me. If I can do all the things they're asking of me, if I can follow all the rules and regulations, I'll benefit spiritually."

But what you discover instead is that rather than all that effort benefiting you, it instead becomes a drain on you. It saps you of spiritual vitality. That's because some of the activities they want you to do are not natural to you; you have to force yourself to do them. And then you aren't good at them, so you struggle with failure, defeat, and frustration.

But you decide to try harder. You determine you're going to do what they say is necessary. But even if you succeed, you're miserable. You've measured up, but you have no joy. You've satisfied their expectations, but you're empty inside. You have a righteousness that comes from keeping the rules, but you're not in love with Christ. There's no gain, only garbage. No real righteousness, only rubbish.

Recognize it for the loss it is. Don't let others define your spiritual life, for you'll miss out on the life Christ wants to give you. Don't let others pressure you into their spiritual lifestyle, or you'll miss out on what life with Christ can really be like.

The goal is to know Christ and be led by him; not a legalistic code but a living Christ. He is the focus point. He is the source. He is your only Lord. Make every effort to know him. Become intimate with him, and he will lead you in the true righteousness that comes from a living faith.

11

ALL I REALLY NEED TO KNOW I LEARNED BY SUFFERING TRIUMPHANTLY UNTIL I DIED

Philippians 3:10–11

Several years ago a popular book came out titled *All I Really Need to Know I Learned in Kindergarten.* In the book, the author writes:

> ALL I REALLY NEED TO KNOW about how to live and what to do and how to be I learned in kindergarten. Wisdom was not at the top of the graduate-school mountain, but there in the sandpile at Sunday School. These are the things I learned.
>
> Share everything.
> Play fair.
> Don't hit people.
> Put things back where you found them.
> Clean up your own mess.
> Don't take things that aren't yours.
> Say you're sorry when you hurt somebody.
> Wash your hands before you eat.
> Flush.
> . . .
> When you go out into the world, watch out for traffic, hold hands, and stick together.[*]

---

[*] Robert L. Fulghum, *All I Really Need to Know I Learned in Kindergarten* (New York: Ballantine Books, 1986), 4–5.

I'm sure that all these things are good to know. They certainly do cover a large part of life. And it's a fun book to read.

But for those of us who are Christians, this list doesn't cover all we need to know. It certainly doesn't cover the most important thing we need to know—the thing we most of all want to know.

I have a friend who lives in Dallas. His name is Bill Lawrence. Bill is one of the most consistently godly men I know. During his life, Bill has let the Lord change him from a brash, insecure, sometimes obnoxious young man into a spiritual leader who now trains other church leaders all over the world. Bill has grown more spiritually during his life than any other person I know. But one night a few years ago, when we were together, Bill said something that struck me and stayed with me. He was commenting on his spiritual life, and he said, "I don't really know the Lord like I want to." My first thought was, "Bill, if you don't know the Lord, none of us do!"

That is the goal, isn't it—to know the Lord. That is what we really need to know—to know Christ. That's the most important thing to know—the thing we most of all want to know. To become so close to him, so intimate with him, that he's a constant presence in our life—to know what he is like, to know what made him act as he did, to know how he thinks about us, to know Christ so completely that we're always interacting with him on something because he's always on our mind, as real to us as any member of our family.

That's what we really need to know—to know Christ.

But we're not there yet. We don't know him as we would like to. There are times when we do grow spiritually, when we come closer to him. Little by little our Christian lives are deepening. But to say that we "know Christ"—well, we don't say that, because something in us says that we don't yet know him as we'd like to, as we sense it's possible to.

How do we get there? How do we get to know him? How do we draw closer to him? How do we become more intimate with him? How do we learn what we really need to know—which is to know Christ?

The apostle Paul pondered that question—"I want to know Christ. What will make that happen?"—and he writes the answer to some dear friends of his in the city of Philippi. He says to them, "I want to know Christ," and then he tells them what will make that happen. He tells us what will get us there. He tells you what will draw you as close to Christ as it is possible to be.

I've tried to capture what he says in the title of this chapter—"All I Really Need to Know I Learned by Suffering Triumphantly Until I Died." The title intrigues me because it sounds so strange. But it's also so very true. All I really need to know—I need to know Christ, I want to know him—I'll learn by suffering triumphantly until I die. That's Paul's thought in Philippians 3:10–11:

> I want to know Christ—yes, to know the power of his resurrection and participation in his sufferings, becoming like him in his death, and so, somehow, attaining to the resurrection from the dead.

"I want to know Christ," Paul says. "And here's what will make that happen: If I can somehow have the power that comes from his resurrection enabling me to live victoriously as I share the kinds of suffering he experienced, and if I can do this to the very end as he did so that I become like him even at the moment of death as I anticipate the resurrection—if I can do this, then I will know him as much as it is possible to know him.

"If I can go through the same sufferings he went through, and if I can triumphantly respond to them with all the power that's available because of his resurrection, and if I can do that to the very end so that when I die my death conforms to his—faithful and submissive to God to the very end—if I can somehow live triumphantly through suffering until the time I die, as I wait for the resurrection, then I will know him."

That's Paul's total thought. Let's look at the individual phrases a bit more closely and ask, "Why is this true? Why is this the way to really know Christ? Why is living triumphantly through suffering until you die the way to know Christ?"

Paul begins, "If you're going to really know Christ, you must first sense 'the power of his resurrection'—the power that comes to you because of his resurrection."

When Christ came up from the dead, that proved that he was the Son of God, that your sins were paid for, and that his Spirit would come inside you and give you the power to live as Christ would live. That's the power that comes to you because of the resurrection.

The resurrection means that Christ is alive and that in some personal way, in Spirit form, he is inside you, prompting you and strengthening you to approach life the way he would approach it. As a result of this internal power, you're able to handle difficult situations without being devastated or defeated. As a result of this power, you're able to triumph through them. So to know Christ, you must first sense the power that comes to you because of his resurrection.

But to really know him, you need to sense this power in specific situations of suffering. That's why Paul goes on say that to really know Christ, you must live triumphantly in his power through the various kinds of suffering Christ went through. If you want to know him, you need to experience the sufferings he experienced and react to them the way he reacted. Look again at his words in verse 10—to know Christ, you must have a "participation in his sufferings." You must know the power of his resurrection as you share his sufferings.

Why is that the case? Why is it necessary to share his sufferings—to suffer what he suffered and respond as he responded—in order to get to know him? Why do we have to live triumphantly through suffering in order to get to know him?

Because—and you've already found this to be true—your greatest spiritual growth has always come when you handled some situation of suffering well. The times when you've had the biggest advances in your spiritual life have always been when you faced something that hurt very badly—a loss of someone or something very dear to you, a betrayal by someone very close to you, an injustice done to you, an overwhelming sorrow that came into your life. If you look back on your life, it was during those times—as God's power was working in you, as his Spirit was producing a godly response in you—it was during those times of triumphing through suffering that you spiritually grew.

I remember my first experience with this. I was in junior high, trying out for the school basketball team. It came down to the final cut, from twenty down to the fifteen that would be on the team. I was among the last five cut.

And I knew I was better than some of those guys that were kept on the team! Later that day, as the sun was setting and as I walked the mile to my home, I had a lot of time to pray. Today, the experience seems inconsequential, but back then I had just lost all the dreams that a junior higher could lose, and my sorrow was crushing. Yet somehow, walking home alone, I was able to turn it over to the Lord and say, "Lord, I believe that you work in all things for good." And that evening, in my young Christian life, I took a small step closer to knowing Christ and being like him.

I've had many chances to say that since then—greater losses, deeper pains, heavier sorrows. Sharing the sufferings of Christ: being rejected by the people I most wanted to minister to, unjust accusations, unfair treatment, isolation, abandonment. And to the degree that his resurrection power enabled me to move through such suffering without becoming bitter, I've learned something of his heart, and I've come to know him better.

Some of you have been rejected by spouses or deserted by boyfriends or girlfriends. Some of you have been kept out of schools you wanted to attend, fired from businesses you gave your heart to, spurned by children you poured your life into, betrayed by people you put your trust in. Some of you have been misunderstood, maligned, and mistreated. And when you realized that Christ also suffered through that, and when you let his power bring a godly response from you, you grew spiritually and came to know him better.

You want to know Christ. And all you ever need in order to know him is to share his sufferings and triumph through his power.

But Paul adds one more thing—becoming like him in his death. "I want to know Christ—yes, the power of his resurrection and participation in his suffering, becoming like him in his death." In other words, "I want that process of suffering triumphantly to continue to the very end, to the moment of death.

"I want my death to be like his. I want to die as he died—faithful and submissive to God to the very end. At the moment of death, I want to go through it as he did—committed to the Father's will, trusting the Father's power. If I can finish like he did, if I experience death the way he experienced it—triumphantly—then I'll know him as much as anyone can. I want to know him to the last degree, and the only way for that to happen is for me to carry it through to the very end."

Some people flake out down the line. They go along well for many years, but then something happens later in life—they do something inexplicable. They make some tragic, unexplainable decision that veers their life away from Christ, hurts those around them, and ends their years with sorrow.

The only way to make sure that doesn't happen is to have a long obedience to the very end, an unending obedience to the last moment of life.

In order for Paul to become like Christ even through the moment of death, he'll obviously have to die and be raised from the dead rather than ascend into heaven alive before dying. He'll have to participate in the resurrection rather than the rapture if he wants that one final opportunity to know Christ better.

That's the meaning of his last line—"becoming like him in his death, and so, somehow, attaining to the resurrection from the dead." He's saying, "I'm ready to be involved in the resurrection instead of the rapture. It's possible Christ could return before I die, and I'd be raptured, caught up alive. And there certainly would be some marvelous benefits to that. But in order to know Christ as intimately, as thoroughly, as completely as I want to, I need to go through death as he died. I need to face execution as he did, and maybe I will since I'll soon stand trial for my life before Caesar. Or maybe I'll die a natural death since I've already told you earlier in my letter that I don't expect the death sentence from this trial. But *somehow*, one way or another, in order to fully know Christ, I need to die and be included in the resurrection rather than be raptured beforehand."

We have been called to a rich life. A life where Christ's triumphant power is available to us. A life where the sins and injustices of the world cannot defeat us. A life that draws us closer and closer to him as we share his sufferings and learn of his heart.

I want to know Christ. All I really need to know I'll learn by suffering triumphantly until I die.

12

STRAINING FOR THE PRIZE

Philippians 3:12–21

I don't watch very much of the Winter Olympics. I can't seem to get interested. My wife and daughters like the figure skating—all that twirling and posing and flowing costumes. I can watch it for a few minutes, but mostly I'm looking to see if someone misses one of those triple spins and splats all over the ice. For me, that kind of makes it interesting because you know they've got to get up, pretend nothing happened, smile, and keep going, all the while thinking, "I'm dead; it's over. What's the point?" I know I'm being a bit morbid, but for me, that's about the only fun in watching figure skating.

I watch another event for a few minutes. A skier on the top of a hill starts down a short run of mounds and dips bunched close across the hill—I think it's called "moguls"—one short dip after another that you bash into as you juggle your way down the hill. You watch the skier go down, knees together, legs pumping in unison, trying to time the dips and mounds as smoothly as possible, getting to the bottom, and you see a time—37.3 seconds. Then you watch another skier do the same thing—same path down, same motions—37.1 seconds. Then another—exactly the same—36.9 seconds. After I watch four or five of them, it seems kind of boring. I know they're racing against the clock, and the fastest time will win a medal. But it's one right after another, all doing the same thing. You've seen one, you've seen them all. Now if two or three of them went down at the same time, and they tried to bump or hip each other and knock each other down as they went, that would make it interesting.

I think maybe that's why I like the Summer Olympics better—they have more head-to-head competition—seven or eight guys or gals on the track all at the same time, racing against each other.

My favorite races are the 220 and the 440—long enough for drama, short enough that the results come fairly quickly. The 220 is halfway around the track, and the 440 is once all the way around the track—both of them short enough to be a sprint all the way and exciting enough because you can see the close finish coming. And the part that always catches my eye— two guys coming down the stretch, running neck and neck, putting everything they've got into it, nearing the tape, and then the last step before the tape, leaning their heads forward, trying to get some part of their body into the tape and across the line, straining the last extra bit to win the prize. For some reason, that makes it interesting—pouring everything into it, pressing every fiber, straining to win the prize.

The Olympic runner straining for the prize—that's the picture in Paul's mind as he writes to some dear friends of his, "I'm straining for the prize. I haven't won it yet, but I'm pressing with every fiber of my being to get it. I'm pouring everything I have into winning it." And then he adds, to them and to us, "Follow my example. You, too, do the same thing. Strain for the prize."

In order to follow Paul's example, we'll need to answer two questions. First, what is the prize? What are we trying to win? What are we trying to take hold of? And then second, how do we strain for it? How do we press toward it? What does that look like? What does that involve?

First, what is the prize? As we read Paul's words, we see that the prize is becoming like Christ. The prize is knowing him and becoming like him.

We aren't there yet. We don't have the prize in our hand yet. But we're pressing toward it; we're straining for it. And one day we'll get it. One day we'll have it. One day, when we're called up to heaven, it will be ours—our transformation will be complete, the process will be finished, and we'll be like him. The prize is being like Christ. We keep straining for it, and someday it'll be ours.

I want to know Christ—yes, to know the power of his resurrection and participation in his sufferings, becoming like him in his death, and so, somehow attaining to the resurrection from the dead.

Not that I have already obtained all this, or have already arrived at my goal, but I press on to take hold of that for which Christ Jesus took hold of me. Brothers and sisters, I do not consider myself yet to have taken hold of it. But one thing I do: Forgetting what is behind and straining toward what is ahead, I press on toward the goal to win the prize for which God has called me heavenward in Christ Jesus. (3:10–14)

Paul is straining to win the prize, which is to know Christ and be like him. When Christ took hold of his life, it was for the purpose of reaching this goal.

Paul hasn't yet reached that goal. "Brothers and sisters, I do not consider myself yet to have taken hold of it. But one thing I do: Forgetting what is behind"—not focusing on how far I've come up to this point, not considering what may have been accomplished so far in my life, but instead—"straining toward what is ahead, I press on toward the goal to win the prize for which God has called me heavenward in Christ Jesus"—the prize of being like him.

All of us who have been Christians for any period of time know this is our goal. Christians may differ on smaller points of doctrine or theology or specific behaviors. And God sorts that out as we go along. But we know one thing for sure—God has called us to be like his Son.

All of us, then, who are mature should take such a view of things. And if on some point you think differently, that too God will make clear to you. Only let us live up to what we have already attained. (3:15–16)

When will we finally get there? When will we finally reach the goal and win the prize? We reach the goal when we're in his presence, when he calls us heavenward. When we're with him in our final home, our transformation will be complete and the process will be finished. And we will have the prize—we will be like him.

But our citizenship is in heaven. And we eagerly await a Savior from there, the Lord Jesus Christ, who, by the power that enables him to bring everything under his control, will transform our lowly bodies so that they will be like his glorious body. (3:20–21)

Our bodies will become like the body he has in glory. And we will be as he is. We will be like Christ—our prize for all eternity.

That's the answer to the first question, "What is the prize?" The prize is to be like Christ. That's what we were called to. That's what Christ took hold of us for—to be like him. We're not there yet. But we press toward it. We strain for it. It happens little by little as we live as he lived. And one day, when he calls us into his presence, the transformation will be complete. And the prize will be ours—we will be like him.

Now for our second question: How do we press toward it? What does it mean to strain for the prize? What does that look like?

We strain for the prize by being obedient even if it means loss or suffering. We obey, even if costs us something. The way we strain for the prize—the way we become like Christ—is by living as he lived, a life focused on the cross, obedient even to the point of death.

That's how Christ lived. He became "obedient to death—even death on a cross" (Phil. 2:8). His life was focused on the cross. And now Paul says, "We strain for the prize, becoming increasingly like Christ, when we, too, obey despite the cost."

A lot of people who call themselves Christians aren't willing to do that. They aren't willing to obey if it's going to cost them. They aren't willing to obey if it's going to cost them a client or a sale. They aren't willing to obey if it's going to cost them a job or a promotion. They aren't willing to obey if it's going to cost them a boyfriend or a girlfriend, if it's going to cost them thousands of dollars in taxes, or if it's going to cost them peace and quiet in the family.

To live a life focused on the cross—willing to obey even though it costs—a lot of people who call themselves Christians aren't willing to do that.

And for them, rather than becoming like Christ, there's a question of whether they really even know him or not, whether they really even belong to him in the first place. They are so opposed to a life focused on the cross, so unwilling to obey if it's going to cost, so antagonistic to that kind of a life that there's a question of whether they really belong to Christ in the first place. They are enemies of the cross. They want nothing to do with that kind of life. And there's a question of whether they're really believers after all.

> For, as I have often told you before and now tell you again even with tears, many live as enemies of the cross of Christ. Their destiny is destruction, their god is their stomach, and their glory is in their shame. Their mind is set on earthly things. (3:18–19)

Some people call themselves Christians, but their entire focus is on "How can I take advantage of and benefit from earthly things? Don't talk to me about obedience that will cost me. I want to focus on what I can get. I prefer to continue what I'm doing. I like what my disobedience brings me now."

"Their god is their stomach"—what's most important to them is whatever will satisfy them physically. That's what they're going to put in first place. They want the higher income and the more pleasurable lifestyle. They want the clothes and the partying. They want to have fun. Their god is their stomach. Rather than the cross—a willingness to obey to the point of cost—their god is whatever will physically satisfy them now.

As a result, they congratulate themselves on things they should be ashamed of. "Their glory is in their shame." They tell themselves they're shrewd because they worked the system, they think they're clever because they pulled a fast one, and they brag how much beer they can hold. They congratulate themselves on things they should be ashamed of.

In their heart, they are enemies of the cross, and their end is destruction. They are far from the heart of Christ. In reality they do not even know him, though they call themselves Christians. They are not headed to heaven; they are headed to hell because everything the cross stands for—obedience unto death for the benefit of others—they have rejected. The cross has had no impact on their lives. They do not know Christ. Their end is destruction.

Paul appeals to us to follow his example instead, as others do:

Join together in following my example, brothers and sisters, and just as you have us as a model, keep your eyes on those who live as we do. (3:17)

My friend, strive for the prize—to be like Christ. Live focused on the cross. Let this be your prayer: "God, as Christ did, I will obey, even to the point of cost."

And when God calls you upward, you will be like him forever.

13

PEACE IN THE CHURCH

Philippians 4:1–9

When I was a pastor in Scottsdale, Arizona, there were two men in the church who were greatly admired. They were successful businessmen and committed to the Lord. Both of them deeply cared to see people come to Christ. Both of them would frequently talk about him with other people during the course of their day. They were widely respected in the church.

One of the men was named Harvey. Harvey owned several steak house restaurants in the area. If you've ever been in the Phoenix–Scottsdale area and you've eaten at Pinnacle Peak—on top of a hill overlooking the city— or at one of the Rusty Nails, you've eaten at one of Harvey's restaurants.

In the early years, Harvey had some partners who turned out to be crooked, and he had to go to court to prevent them from stealing the businesses from him. During those months he and I used to meet for breakfast every couple of weeks at 6:30 in the morning just for encouragement and so that somebody would know what he was going through. One time, early in the morning at the restaurant, after we'd been meeting at 6:30 for about four to five months, he said, "My wife wants to know: do you get up this early every day, or do you think I get up this early every day?" But during those tough years he walked faithfully with God, and he left a good testimony in the courts and the community.

After I had been gone for about twenty years, the Scottsdale church asked if I would help out with the preaching for a few months. For several months I flew from California to Phoenix on weekends. One Sunday, I mentioned in the service that the next week my whole family would be there.

It had been twenty years since the kids had been in Scottsdale. Though the church had grown from six hundred to several thousand in those years, there were still lots of people who remembered the kids from when they were little, and I thought they would enjoy seeing what they looked like grown up. Plus, my kids, some of whom were now married, wanted to show their spouses the Scottsdale home they'd grown up in and the church.

At the end of that service, Harvey came to the front, where I was talking with some people, and waited until I had finished some conversations with others. When I saw him—"Harvey, how are you?"

"Good. It's good to see you, Don. How long is your family going to be here next week?"

"Just for the weekend. We're flying in mid-day Friday, and we'll fly out Sunday night."

"Do you think they'd enjoy an evening at Pinnacle Peak as my guests?" And I suddenly realized what he was offering me—a gift of expensive steak dinners for all fifteen of us at a spectacular outdoor eating spot, complete with the band entertainment and everything. I was dumbfounded but managed to say, "Harvey, they would love it. That would be great. Thanks." When we arrived at Pinnacle Peak Saturday night, the manager was expecting us. We had a special table waiting. Two waitresses were exclusively assigned to us. We could order anything and everything off the menu that we wanted—appetizers, desserts, T-bones, filets—my kids were so impressed that I knew the owner of the place and that he would freely give us all these things!

That was Harvey—a generous, godly man, whose restaurants were famous in the city.

The second greatly admired man in the church was Tom. Tom moved to Scottsdale and started attending the church after I'd been the pastor there for about four to five years. Tom had had a successful business back in the Midwest, but he had sold it in order to move to Arizona and be in charge of the "I Found It" campaign that Campus Crusade was putting on nationwide. You may remember that campaign. Bright yellow bumper stickers with blue letters appeared on the back of all the Christians' cars in the city saying "I Found It!" Billboards around town—same bold letters, same exclamation point—"I Found It!" But nothing ever said what the "It" was. Everywhere you drove—"I Found It!" "I Found It!" "I Found It!"—but the people in the city had no idea what "It" was. Meanwhile, all the churches were going through extensive telephone training because we were heading toward a time when we were going to call every home in the city and say, "Have you noticed the 'I Found It!' stickers and billboards around town?" "Yeah, what's it about?" And if the person was interested, that would lead into a guided conversation about how we'd found Christ as the answer to our deepest needs in life. Thousands of people came to Christ during that campaign.

All the churches of Phoenix and Scottsdale—all the churches in the whole state of Arizona—were mobilized for this advertising campaign and telephone conversation. And Tom had sold his business and moved his wife and five children to Arizona in order to donate two years of his life to make all this happen statewide for Campus Crusade.

I once asked him, "Tom, what made you sell everything, liquidate everything, and live off your savings for a couple of years in a state you'd never been to?" His answer: "The challenge. Bill Bright, the director of Campus Crusade, put the challenge to me, and I felt this was something God wanted me to do." I was impressed; he had sold everything and moved across the country to serve Christ for free.

Two men in the church, both greatly admired. Successful businessmen, both committed to the Lord. The biggest thing in both of their lives was seeing other people come to Christ. Godly men, well respected in the church.

When the "I Found It" campaign was over, Tom was ready to get back into business and start earning income again after living off of his savings for two years. And he and Harvey got together. Harvey was building some additional restaurants, and he hired Tom to oversee the construction process.

Something happened where the construction costs drastically increased beyond what was expected. Harvey was disturbed at how much additional money it was now costing and was making some questioning comments about Tom's handling of things. Tom felt he was being criticized and blamed for mismanagement, and he was making comments back about "sticking with your side of the business and not poking in where you don't know what you are talking about."

The whole situation got a bit edgy, and people in the church began to pick up on the tension. Harvey and Tom avoided each other at church. None of us had enough information to know what the real facts were. All we knew was that it was awkward for us to see them acting that way toward each other. All I could say to them was, "Hey, guys, when the giants fight, the whole church trembles." Eventually they worked at it to get some peace between them, but it meant that Tom quit working for Harvey.

Two men in the church, both greatly admired. Godly men, well respected. And yet, something caused a tension between them. Sometimes that happens. Sometimes even godly, committed Christians "get on the outs" with each other. Lots of understandable things can make it happen.

Maybe their kids date for a period of time, but then one of them breaks ups with the other, and the other family wonders, "My kid wasn't good enough for you?"

Maybe the church is ready to support one of the church families for several thousand dollars for a five-week summer mission project in Romania, but at the last minute, one of the board members convinces the rest of the board that an AIDS project in Africa needs the money more desperately. And the family wonders if there was something personal in his argument to turn the money from them towards the AIDS project.

Maybe one man teaches in his Sunday school class that it's all right to have a glass of wine with a meal. Another man in the class is terribly disturbed at hearing this said to others. This other man grew up in an alcoholic home. He saw his father come home many nights dead drunk and saw him beat his mother. And if he tried to step in to help his mother, his dad would smash him out of the way. To him, there's nothing more dangerous or damaging than to tell people they can drink. He brings up his objection in the class. The teacher defends his viewpoint. The second man gets more heated in arguing, maybe calling the teacher "irresponsible." The teacher maybe answers back that he's being "legalistic." And suddenly both men find themselves in a tense relationship with each other.

Maybe a woman has planned the Christmas decorations for the church every year for the past ten years. She starts her planning in October every year—thinking up a theme, involving people in creating banners and decorations to fit the theme, going into the mountains with her husband to cut a fresh tree, and spending hours in early December arranging and setting everything up just perfectly. And every year the people in the church are just amazed and appreciative. And the woman feels that this is her ministry—this is the way she serves and blesses the church each year.

But one year her elderly mother is diagnosed with cancer and given five months to live. The woman moves her mother into her home in September and begins to provide almost round-the-clock care for her for the next five months. Everyone in the church sees her love for her mother and admires her. They know she simply won't have time to handle the Christmas decorations this year, and they all understand. Some other lady volunteers to handle it, and it turns out fine. But the following year the woman who's been doing it for ten years discovers that this other lady has started early to plan the decorations again, and suddenly she realizes that the other lady is assuming that she'll handle the decorations now each year, instead of it coming back to her. And she's hurt, and offended, and understandably put out.

Sometimes something happens where even godly, committed Christians "get on the outs" with each other. It's not hard to see how this happens.

But when it does, the rest of the church is affected. Others become aware of the tension. They see the avoidance. And a big elephant enters into the church. It isn't really anybody's fault, but it's there in the room, and nobody's quite sure how to deal with it, least of all the people who are involved. And instead of there being a deep peace in the church, there's a sense of walking on eggshells, an unease and a strain.

What can be done to bring peace back into the church? What can be done to restore that wonderful peace to the people involved and to the church as a whole? How can the "peace of God" come back into their hearts toward each other, and how can the "God of peace" envelop the church again?

Paul found himself faced with just such a situation in the church that was closest to his heart. He loved them more than he loved any church. They had responded to his ministry when he was in their city. They had supported him financially when he left. They had sent people and funds to take care of him when he was arrested. And they were doing their best to stand firm in their Christianity against a hostile culture, so he writes a letter to encourage them.

But as he comes to the end of his letter, he knows there's an elephant in the church. The church doesn't have peace because they're not sure what to do about the awkward tension between two of their members. Two godly ladies in the church have some issue that has gotten between them. They don't know how to get past it so that they themselves can have peace and so that God's peace can return to the church.

And so Paul writes to help them. And what he says will also help us, for he tells us what to do when we're on the outs with another brother or sister so that the "peace of God" can return to our hearts and the "God of peace" can again settle on the church.

After reminding the church how much he loves them, Paul brings up the elephant in the room—his two dear friends who have some issue between them:

> Therefore, my brothers and sisters, you whom I love and long for, my joy and crown, stand firm in the Lord in this way, dear friends!
>
> I plead with Euodia and I plead with Syntyche to be of the same mind in the Lord. Yes, and I ask you, my true companion, help these women since they have contended at my side in the cause of the gospel, along with Clement and the rest of my coworkers, whose names are in the book of life. (4:1–3)

Two ladies who are giants in the church. Two ladies who worked with Paul harder than anyone to spread the gospel. They "contended at my side in the cause of the gospel," he says. But some issue, some tension, has entered their relationship. Paul doesn't mention what the specific issue is, but obviously everybody in the church knows.

Paul pleads with his two dear friends to come to some harmony on the matter. He even asks another respected leader in the church—some "true companion"—to help them work it out. And then in the verses that follow, verses 4–9, he reveals what we should do so that the "peace of God" can return to us and the "God of peace" can be with the church.

First, he says, turn your thoughts to the fact that the Lord could soon be coming for you. As that thought fills your mind, the issue between you won't matter so much, and you'll find yourself more gentle and forbearing with each other. Preoccupy yourself with the Lord, and let the thought of his any-moment coming so overwhelm you that the concern between the two of you takes on a secondary importance.

> *Rejoice in the Lord always. I will say it again: Rejoice! Let your gentleness be evident to all. The Lord is near.* (4:4–5)

"Rejoice in the Lord." Take your joy in the Lord. Turn your thoughts to him. "The Lord is near." He's coming soon for you. At any moment he's going to call you upward. And he's going to change you into being like him for all eternity. That's what's ahead for you. As you fully absorb that, this issue won't seem like such a big deal to you.

Right now, the issue hurts and frustrates and agitates. It seems to have consequences. It seems to affect other things that are important.

But if you focus on what really matters, what's really ahead for you—the Lord is coming—the issue will take on its true lesser importance, and you'll find yourself more gentle and tolerant of one another. Instead of chafing and resenting and wanting to snap back at each other, the truth of the Lord's coming overwhelms you and enables you to handle the tension with patience and forbearance.

"Rejoice in the Lord. I say it again: Focus on him. He could be coming very soon." That's the first step to having peace come into your heart—preoccupy yourself with the Lord's coming, and let that produce a softer spirit toward the other person.

The second step—whatever concerns you still may have about the issue—is to turn it over to the Lord. Whatever importance you think it still has, talk to the Lord about it. Tell him what bothers you about it. Lay the issue out before him. Ask him for what you think would be right in the matter.

Focusing on the Lord's coming causes your spirit to become more gentle and accepting, but you still may have concerns about how the incident might affect you or the church. So put the matter in the Lord's hands. Ask him to act in the situation and resolve the matter. And the peace that you want will come to you:

Do not be anxious about anything, but in every situation, by prayer and petition, with thanksgiving, present your requests to God. And the peace of God, which transcends all understanding, will guard your hearts and your minds in Christ Jesus. (4:6–7)

"Do not be anxious about anything." Don't fret and stew over it. Did somebody act insensitively during the breakup with your child? Are the elders making a decision with the money that's against the best interest of the church? Is the Sunday school teacher off base in what he's teaching? Don't I do the Christmas decorations in a grand way every year? How come others don't see things the way I see them?

Don't let your concern lead to frustration or anxiety. Lay the issue out before God. Ask him for what you think would be right. "In every situation, by prayer and petition, with thanksgiving, present your requests to God."

Four words here—*prayer, petition, requests,* and *thanksgiving. Prayer:* "Lord, I'm going to approach you; I'm going to talk to you about it." *Petition:* "I'm going to ask for your help. I need you to intervene." *Requests:* "Lord, here are the specifics; here are the particulars that concern me."

Prayer, petition, requests—with *thanksgiving.* "I'm thankful that you know what's best; you know what should be done. I'm thankful that you're in control and that you can make your will be done."

What would that sound like? "In every situation, by prayer and petition, with thanksgiving, present your requests to God." It might sound something like this.

"God, my daughter is hurting because the boy from the other family broke up with her. Lord, I don't know if the other parents put pressure on their son because they didn't think my daughter was good enough for him. I don't know. Lord, help me not to be anxious or upset about this. Help me to think rightly about this. Maybe this is your goodness to my child. Maybe you're protecting her from an unwise choice down the line. Maybe you have someone very specific and very good in mind that you're bringing to her, and you needed to have her open and available and looking. God, I thank you for your love to our family in the past. I thank you that you're a God who only does good."

"God, the church undid their support to us for the summer missions project in Romania. They promised us several thousand dollars, and now it's going instead to AIDS relief in Africa. Lord, we went through a lot of preparation for this trip. We went to some classes, we cleared our calendars, we got some shots. We were really looking forward to this. I saw it as a great family time. And Lord, I also saw it as a chance for my kids to see your reality and power in ways they've never seen before. They would see that you're a big God and that they were going to be connected to you for the rest of their lives. Lord, at the last minute the church money is gone, and I don't have personal funds to handle the trip. Does the church not have confidence in us? Do they not think it would be a good expenditure? Is that why they took it away from us? Lord, help me not to get anxious or tied up in knots over this. Do you have a reason why you don't want us overseas this summer? Is there some physical or health danger you're protecting us from? Do you know something about my business—that there's some reason why I need to be in the states this summer for my business' sake? Are you sparking some breakthrough against AIDS in Africa, where there's going to be a tremendous release of compassion and help, and revival will sweep through the continent? God, I thank you that you see the future in ways I don't. You see ripples and ramifications that I can never see. I thank you that you're the God of the nations and the God of our family."

"God, Bill kind of attacked me in Sunday school over this alcohol thing. Lord, his hostility seemed out of proportion to the issue. Have I offended him in some way? Is he looking for some excuse just to butt heads with me and get back at me for something I may have done to him? Lord, I don't want to impugn wrong motives to him if there aren't any. Help me not to overreact or obsess on this. Was I insensitive to his background, to his family history? Was I arrogant and prideful in my teaching—'I know the truth, and I'm going to show you my superior biblical knowledge'? Lord, do I need to be more gentle and humble in my teaching? Is this a situation where I need to go to Bill and ask for his forgiveness—not for what I said but for how I said it? God, I thank you that you're a God who probes our hearts and that you continually draw us to become more like your Son. I thank you for showing me my pride, and I thank you for all the good things Bill does in this church."

"God, nobody said anything about my doing the Christmas decorations this year. Everybody seems to assume that this other lady is going to do them from now on. Lord, I've been doing them for ten years, and I've loved it. Lord, it hurts; I feel unappreciated. Did they not like what I was doing? Did they not know how to say that to me, and is this their indirect way of easing me out? Lord, I don't want to fret or get upset over this. Help me to look at this clearly. Is it possible, Lord, that I've really run out of good ideas and that a person with a fresh approach will be good for the church? Is it that you have some other major task you want me to give my energy to, and I'd never see it if I still had this other responsibility? Are you doing something in this other lady's life? Is this the first time in her life that she's excited about what she's doing for you? Does she need this in her life more than I do—to confirm her love for your people and her willingness to serve them in any way that will help? God, I thank you that you're a God who can draw all hearts to you. I thank you that you're a God who provides for his church in generation after generation and that in each new decade and generation, you raise up others to bless your people."

Prayer: "God, I don't want to be anxious about this. I come to you." *Petition*: "I need your help." *Requests*: "Here are the specific issues to help me sort through this." With *thanksgiving*: "I'm grateful that you know things I don't know and that I can trust you to do good."

When you find yourself "on the outs" with another believer, preoccupy yourself with the realization that the Lord is coming, and let that foster a greater gentleness toward them. Then talk to the Lord about it. Lay the matter out before him, asking for what you need and thanking him for who he is. And you will find that God's unexplainable peace will simply overwhelm you and penetrate deep within.

> *Rejoice in the Lord always. I will say it again: Rejoice! Let your gentleness be evident to all. The Lord is near. Do not be anxious about anything, but in every situation, by prayer and petition, with thanksgiving, present your requests to God. And the peace of God, which transcends all understanding, will guard your hearts and your minds in Christ Jesus. (4:4–7)*

God's peace will protect your heart and guard your mind. That's how the *peace of God* comes to you.

And how does the *God of peace* descend on the church? How does the God of peace then permeate every area of the church and become settled among us?

As the peace of God descends on individuals, the God of peace then descends on the church as the rest of the congregation is now able to attend to all the things that are good and right and pure. The church can now concentrate on all the excellent things God has for us, the things that are worthy of praise. That's how Paul concludes:

> *Finally, brothers and sisters, whatever is true, whatever is noble, whatever is right, whatever is pure, whatever is lovely, whatever is admirable—if anything is excellent or praiseworthy—think about such things. Whatever you have learned or received or heard from me, or seen in me—put it into practice. And the God of peace will be with you.* (4:8–9)

The *peace of God* enters our hearts, and the *God of peace* descends on the church.

There's a little poem I heard a long time ago. It goes something like this:

> To live above, with saints we love,
>> O, that will be glory.
> But to live below with saints we know,
>> Well, that's another story.

If I were writing that poem today for my church, I think I'd write it this way:

> To live above, with saints we love,
>> Yes, that will be glory.
> To live below with saints we know.
>> That, too, is a wonderful story.

14

HOW SHOULD A PASTOR THINK ABOUT HIS PEOPLE'S GIVING?

Philippians 4:10–23

At a recent lunch with some pastors, something caused me to mention my title for this chapter to the group—"How Should a Pastor Think About His People's Giving?" A pastor of a fairly large church sitting kitty-corner from me leaned back in his chair and laughed. "At my church, they would probably edit that to read 'Should a Pastor Think About His People's Giving?'" The pastor next to me chimed in, "Some churches would say, 'Dare a Pastor Think About His People's Giving?'" And everyone laughed.

But it's obvious that pastors do think about their people's giving. And if you listen to them talk or preach about it, you can easily figure out what their thinking is.

If they harangue or make long drawn-out appeals, if they brow-beat people or use guilt to manipulate, then it's obvious what their thoughts are: they think their people are reluctant to give and that they have to be pressured or subjected to "stewardship programs" every year in order to pry the money out of them.

If they publicly record donation amounts in the bulletin or in some event program—"so-and-so donated or pledged this much"—then they think people will only give if they get some recognition for it.

If they plan raffles, bingo, or other fund-raising activities, then it's apparent they think people will only give if they get something back for it or have a chance to win even more in return.

Some pastors think you should first give ten percent of your income to their church—and that any giving to other organizations should only be after you've first given ten percent to the church.

It's obvious that pastors do think about their people's giving, and if you listen to them, you can figure out what their thoughts are.

But that still leaves the question of what their thoughts should be. How should pastors think about their people's giving? What ought to be in their minds?

We get some answers to this question from the end of a letter Paul wrote to his friends in the city of Phillipi. They had just sent him a rather substantial gift to support him while he was under house arrest in Rome. The rent on the house and his food was his responsibility. Unless he was able to pay it, he would be put in a dungeon while he waited for his trial and fed any slop that was available. So the gift was helpful and meant a lot.

They had sent the money with one of their church members—Epaphroditus. It had been a hard trip, eight hundred miles, with primitive transportation. Epaphroditus had almost died getting the money to Paul. But now he was well enough to return home, and he was going to take Paul's letter with him.

And so at the end of the letter, before he signs off and gives it to Epaphroditus, Paul writes a few lines to thank them for their gift. And from what he writes, we learn how a pastor ought to think about his people's giving.

First, a pastor should be glad for his people's giving, but not because it's meeting a need in the ministry or because the ministry is dependent on it. The truth is, their giving is not critical to the ministry. God can continue the ministry whether they give or not. That's the first thing Paul says—"I rejoice at your giving, but not because it's meeting some need":

> *I rejoiced greatly in the Lord that at last you renewed your concern for me. Indeed, you were concerned, but you had no opportunity to show it. I am not saying this because I am in need, for I have learned to be content whatever the circumstances. I know what it is to be in need, and I know what it is to have plenty. I have learned the secret of being content in any and every situation, whether well fed or hungry, whether living in plenty or in want. I can do all this through him who gives me strength.* (4:10–13)

When Paul says he's pleased that they have renewed their concern for him, he uses a word that refers to a flower blooming again—it renews its display, like a perennial that comes back every year, blossoming again. They have renewed; they have acted again on their concern for him.

This particular church had given Paul money on several occasions. The first time he came to their city, he had brought the gospel to them. When he was getting ready to leave for another city, they sent him on his way with a good sum of money. They followed that up over the months and years with repeated gifts, continuing to support him in his teaching and travels. In fact, they were the only church to support him financially.

But something interrupted that pattern. It wasn't that their concern or desire stopped, but something interfered with their ability to act on it. There was a period of time when they weren't able to display that concern. Paul doesn't say why; he only says in verse 10: "Indeed, you have been concerned, but you had no opportunity to show it." It might be that they went through a tough time financially and didn't have the money to send. Or it might be that they simply lost touch with Paul. He moved around a lot. Communication depended on travelers bringing information. It was hard to stay current with where people were or what they were up to. But once they had word that he was under an extended house arrest in Rome, they immediately sent Epaphroditus with money to help.

"I'm glad," he says, "that you have again showed your concern for me." Why? Not because their gift met some need that he might have. He explains what he means.

There had been times in his life when he was aware that he had needs. There were other times in his life when he realized he actually had plenty. But he found that neither condition seemed to affect him that much. One way or another, his circumstances were not a major factor in his life. Instead, his internal stability and contentment remained pretty much the same whether he was missing a few meals or whether he had a refrigerator full of food. That was because he had discovered that something much more powerful was driving his life—an internal, compelling strength that was independent of his financial circumstances. Christ was inside him, moving his life forward, and these externals were of secondary concern. Because of this internal strengthening, he could contentedly live in any set of circumstances.

How should a pastor think about his people's giving? He should be glad for it, but not because it meets some need in the ministry. He should be glad, but not because the ministry is dependent on it. The truth is, their giving is not critical to the ministry. God can continue the ministry whether they give or not.

The ministry might have more funds or less funds to work with, but something much more powerful than money is at the center of ministry. The driving force of ministry is Christ. The strengthening power of ministry is Christ. And whether the funds are great or small, Christ can move his work forward.

That's where a pastor's thinking ought to start—God has a ministry for us to do regardless of the level of our income. The church might feel the pinch and the pain, or it might feel flush and full. But what matters is that Christ is in the people, and he can move his ministry forward regardless of what the finances are.

Well, if a pastor is glad for their giving, but not because it meets a need, then why is he glad? What thought is in the pastor's mind that makes him glad if it's not that the ministry now has more money? Paul says, "I rejoice greatly—but not because it met a need." Then what is the reason he's glad?

That brings us to the second thought that a pastor should have about his people's giving.

He should be glad for their giving, not because it meets a need in the ministry but because it tells him something about his people. It tells him that they view themselves as partners in the ministry. They see themselves as sharing the ministry with him. He's glad because they care as much about the ministry as he does. That's Paul's point in verses 14–16: "I rejoice greatly, because it shows me that you share in the ministry with me."

Yet it was good of you to share in my troubles. Moreover, as you Philippians know, in the early days of your acquaintance with the gospel, when I set out from Macedonia, not one church shared with me in the matter of giving and receiving, except you only; for even when I was in Thessalonica, you sent me aid more than once when I was in need. (4:14–16)

Twice in these verses he speaks of their "sharing" in the ministry: "It was good of you to share in my troubles; not one church shared with me in the matter of giving and receiving, except you only." What made him glad was not the amount of the money but the evidence that they were committed. They, too, had ownership of his ministry. What made him glad was that they felt that they were sharing in what God was doing through him.

I remember when I was pastoring in Austin, Texas. Some years before I got there, the church had bought four acres and built a classroom–office building with the intention of building a sanctuary somewhere down the line. But over the years it became obvious that the four acres would be woefully inadequate for the church's ministry. The city code would not allow them to build the sanctuary since the small land size wouldn't provide sufficient parking spaces.

After I had been there a few years, the decision was made to sell the four-acre site and find a larger piece of land. The church identified the new site, wrote a preliminary contract on it, and then began the process of seeking funds from the people to finish the purchase. Different people gave different amounts as they were able. I learned that one particular individual—a medical doctor—sold a building he owned and gave the entire proceeds—$100,000—to the church. Without any fanfare, he put a good-sized dent in his retirement in order to help God's work move forward.

And my thinking wasn't: "Wow, $100,000. This will really go a long way. This will help us get the new land!" No. My first thought was: "Man, Joe really believes in this church. He really wants it to do God's work. He owns it as much as I do. This matters to him."

We don't support God's ministry. We share in it. God's ministry does not depend on our support. But if you would like to share in it with God, he'll let you. And when a pastor sees that spirit in his people—that they want to share in the ministry—he's glad.

There's a third thought a pastor should have about his people's giving. When he sees his people giving, he knows they're growing spiritually. He knows their godliness is advancing. Their relationship with Christ is continuing to progress. That's what Paul says next—"I'm not looking for the money; I'm looking to see that your spiritual account is growing":

Not that I desire your gifts; what I desire is that more be credited to your account. (4:17)

"I'm looking at your spiritual account, and I see more being credited or added to it. I see increasing spiritual capital or profit in your account. I see that godliness is growing in your life."

It's like when you get a quarterly statement on your investments, your IRA, or your portfolio. You compare the end of the last quarter with the results of the current quarter, and you see that your account is growing! More has been credited to your account—additional deposits, matches by your employer, an accrual of interest, compound growth. The gain is apparent!

When a pastor looks at his people's giving, he sees the same thing—"Look at the greater godliness in their lives! Their spiritual growth is apparent. Their intimacy with God, their relationship with Christ—what a tremendous gain has taken place!" When a pastor thinks about his people's giving, his thought should be, "How godly they are becoming!"

Why is that true? Why should their giving convince him of their godliness? What is there about their generous giving that tells him they have a growing walk with Christ?

Because he knows that when people give money, it's because God has become more important to them than the money. When he sees them giving their money, he knows that in their thinking, God matters more to them than what the money could do for them.

"Could the money do something for me in the future? Yes. It could provide for a nice retirement. I need security. Money is certainly important for that. But is God more important than that? Which has the most influence on my security—money or God? Which is the biggest factor in determining my security—money or God? Which one has the most control over what my future will be like—money or God?"

Obviously, we are encouraged to plan for our future. But the one who gives generously and trusts his financial future to God shows that his spiritual account is growing because God is becoming a bigger factor in his life.

"Could the money buy something for me right now? Yes. It could buy a nicer car. It could buy a house. It could buy a vacation overseas. It could buy a digital camera. It could buy a lot of things. But do huge amounts of my money go first to those things or first to the things of God? Which comes first—what my money will do for me or what my money will do for God? Which one is most important to me—buying or giving?"

And when a pastor sees that giving comes first, he knows that the hearts of his people are moving toward Christ. They're growing spiritually.

A pastor should be glad for his people's giving, not because it's meeting a need in the ministry but rather because it shows that they see themselves as partners sharing in the ministry and because it shows that they are growing spiritually.

And then the final thought: he should be glad because he knows what God is going to do for them in return. He knows their giving is a sweet aroma that ascends to God, a fragrance that comes into his presence and so delights him that he turns to see who is responsible, and then says to them, "I will take care of all your needs." When a pastor thinks about his people's giving, he should be glad for he knows that his God will see that they lack for nothing:

> I have received full payment and have more than enough. I am amply supplied, now that I have received from Epaphroditus the gifts you sent. They are a fragrant offering, an acceptable sacrifice, pleasing to God. And my God will meet all your needs according to the riches of his glory in Christ Jesus. (4:18–19)

Paul says in verse 18, "I am amply supplied." In other words, "I have all that I need." And then two sentences later, at the end of verse 19, in his language, he repeats the same word—"I am *supplied*, and now my God will *supply* all you need. You have amply supplied God's ministry, and now God, out of his wealth, will meet every need you have."

Paul received their gifts, not as a paid preacher but as a privileged priest, to offer them as a fragrant sacrifice to God. And he knew that God was going to give them even more in return.

Give generously. Not because the ministry needs it but because you want to share in what God is doing and because you want God to become big in your life. And you will discover how incredibly rich God will be toward you!